HIS LORDSHIP'S OBEDIENT SERVANT

The author (age 9) with brother Gwyn on left and Vivian in centre

His Lordship's Obedient Servant

Recollections of a South Wales Borderer

Arthur Herbert Jones

Gomer Press
1987

First publication — April 1987

ISBN 0 86383 299 7

© Arthur Herbert Jones

Printed by J. D. Lewis & Sons Ltd.,
Gomer Press, Llandysul, Dyfed

To my grandchildren John, Rupert, Anthony
and William and to the memory of Roy,
another much loved grandson, whose absence
is deeply felt

Contents

LIST OF ILLUSTRATIONS OTHER THAN LINE DRAWINGS

The line drawings illustrating stories in Part 1, with the exception of that showing Nantyceisiad Farmhouse, were provided by the author's grandson, John Stringer. That of the farmhouse was drawn by John's brother, Roy, an architect, shortly before his death in November 1985, age 25, in a car accident.

Introduction

This collection of stories of my boyhood and of my experiences as a private secretary ending, for reasons of propriety, fifty years ago (together with the short biographies of two men related to me who, unlike myself, had adventurous lives) has been put together with the encouragement of friends who had read some of my shorter pieces of autobiography.

Until my retirement from full-time employment in 1972 at the age of seventy, I had written only two stories. In 1957 The Milk Producer, the journal of the Milk Marketing Board, had welcomed my story about Caerphilly cheese (can any subject be less romantic and offer less scope for exciting adventure?); about the same time the Western Mail published an account of an incident drawn from my electioneering experiences in Cardiff's Tiger Bay area in 1918, now more fully described in 'Yes, I was a Yesman'.

In 1980, the editor of Y Drych (The Mirror), a Welsh American monthly newspaper published in Wisconsin, invited suggestions for improving that newspaper, which, after more than a century, had gone into what seemed to be an irreversible decline. With what I hope was an uncharacteristic lack of modesty, I wrote and sent off some boyhood reminiscences and, later, the life stories of two great uncles, the brothers John and William Davies, were published.

The story of William Davies, 'Texan Shepherd,' came to the notice of Dr. Escal F. Duke, formerly Professor of History at the University of San Angelo, Texas, who asked me to reduce it to the length of a paper which he would read at a meeting of the West Texas Historical Association. I do so, and the paper was duly read by him and appeared in the 1982 edition of the Association's Year Book.

Thus encouraged, I wrote 'Yes, I was a Yesman' from notes made many years earlier and 'His Lordship's Obedient Servant,' two pieces of autobiography covering the years 1918-23 and 1927-34 respectively. These have not yet appeared in print either here or in the U.S.A.

Those stories left a gap between them of four years about which I had intended to say nothing. They were unhappy years which I have tried to forget, but feeling that I had to say all or nothing I wrote 'Strange Interlude.'

I wish to acknowledge the help I have received from the following: my cousin, Jocelyn Davies, for allowing me to use the letters sent home by John and William Davies, Dr. Escal F. Duke, for his research in western Texas where he discovered the site of the Davies homestead and the extent of the Davies ranch, my grandsons John and Roy Stringer, for their line drawings illustrating stories of my boyhood and, especially, Miss Cathryn Gwynn of the Gomer Press for her advice and encouragement, without which this book would not have appeared.

Part I

The Land of My Fathers
1902 - 1918

By Mountain Path to School

The large school bus stopped in front of my bedroom window. It did so often on that narrow country road to allow oncoming traffic to pass, but if I saw it there I gave it no thought. That morning it was different. Convalescent after a long illness I was sitting up in bed taking breakfast and I had a chance to observe the young passengers on their way from a neighbouring village to the large Comprehensive School down the road. 'Lucky beggars,' I said to myself as with self-pity I recalled my own journeyings to and from school at their age. The distance I had to cover was twice that of the boys and girls in the bus and involved the ascent and descent of a mountain.

During that short stop I had had time to note that the children in the bus, or at least the boys, were either fooling about or sitting looking bored. Bored? I had never been bored on my journeys to and from school: instead, as season succeeded season I had found the walk interesting as well as challenging. And recalling the sights, sounds and scents that had accompanied me on that twice-daily trudge over the mountain, I came in time to realize that what over the intervening fifty years I had regarded as a deprivation in my supposedly 'disadvantaged and under-privileged' early years, had really been a blessing on which I could rightly congratulate myself. I had been the 'lucky beggar.'

Before retracing those steps I should explain, perhaps, how it came about that I had to take so arduous a route to school. Seventy-one years ago, that is, during the First World War, I was living at Machen, a large village in the Rhymney valley in Gwent, eight miles from Newport. My mother's brothers, uncles Tom and Jack, living in the same village some years earlier had won scholarships to Newport High School and had travelled there by train. I had sat the same exam, but had failed to win a place at Newport High and was offered instead a place at a Monmouthshire County School, Pontywaun County (now defunct) at Risca, over the mountain in the Ebbw valley, a school with a much lower status, both socially and educationally.

That failure to get into Newport High had been attributed by my parents to my dullness or laziness and they looked upon my walk over the mountain as a just punishment. I had shared their view and trace my change of attitude to the day I saw and thought about the bored boys in the bus.

Nothing, I now feel, could have been better for me in the three years between my thirteenth and sixteenth birthdays than having twice daily a mountain to climb, pure mountain air to breathe and magnificent views to enjoy, mostly rural and industrialized only sufficiently to lend interest to the scene and not to mar it! For this was Mynydd Machen, from whose slopes W. H. Davies, the Welsh tramp-poet, might well have written—for nowhere else in Gwent would offer a better vantage point:

> 'Where from the hills of Gwent
>   I saw the earth
> Burned into two by Severn's silver flood.'

Leaving home about eight o'clock, my way first led past a small plantation of pines, my playground on summer evenings, to a foot-bridge spanning the Brecon and Merthyr Railway (known to us boys as the Breakneck and Murder Railway), then through a small wood to a gate in the mountain wall and so on to the stony mountain path.

Tall bracken in summer bordered the path to begin with, giving way as I climbed to stunted bracken interspersed with grass, reed and patches of heather near the one thousand foot contour line. Around me were the mountain sheep and, apart from their cries and, in spring, the shriller and more plaintive calls of their lambs, the only common sounds were the songs of skylarks and the puffing and clanking of the coal trains as they made their way down the valley to the port of Newport. Birds were everywhere, from hovering hawks to tiny wrens, beautiful yellow-hammers among them, as were a great profusion of butterflies. It was a naturalist's paradise.

In a quarter of an hour I would be high above the village, with its church spire and four chapels standing head and shoulders above the cottages with their smoking chimneys. In a few minutes more, were I to look back, Caerphilly with its large, grey castle, dominating not only the small town but also the wide valley, would come within sight, while immediately opposite me and on the other side of the winding river, the farms and woods of Lord Tredegar's Estate added interest as well as beauty to the ever widening view as season followed season.

Higher still, the panorama extended to bring into sight behind the Ruperra Castle woods the smoking stacks of the Cardiff steelworks and, beyond them, Penarth Head with its St. Augustine's church standing out prominently, a landmark both for mariners and landsmen.

To the east of Cardiff a more exciting prospect would open up before me—a long stretch of the Bristol Channel (W. H. Davies's 'silver

16

flood'), dotted with steamers on their way to and from Bristol and Newport and backed by the Mendip Hills of Somerset, with Clevedon and Weston-Super-Mare sometimes easily discernible, while on the flat moors in the middle distance the progress of smoke trails from engines on the Great Western Railway would tell me whether I was watching an express or goods train.

Ships coming from and going to all parts of the world and express trains to London (a city which I and most people in Machen had never seen). What an exciting prospect for a boy with imagination on his way to and from school!

Then, on the plateau that marked the summit of my climb, the massive towers of Newport's famous transporter bridge would come into sight and ahead, on the far side of the Ebbw valley, Twyn Barlwm mountain, with its large tumulus (known locally as the 'tump') provided both beauty and prehistoric significance to the scene.

Here, on the plateau, the stony path gave way to short springy turf, whereon, had I been hurrying (and I was usually late and in a hurry) I would tend to slow down 'to get my breath back.' Two features on the small plateau, one natural and eternal, the other man-made and pathetically temporal, I have never forgotten.

Rising out of the grass and bracken a short distance from my path was a mass of stones, granite-like in hardness and grey in colour, but containing a large quantity of quartz that glinted in the sun, making them unlike any other stones in the area. This, I had learned at school, was an outcrop of rock usually found below the coal seams that also came to the surface near that spot. When younger, I had preferred the local legend that this was where 'the devil broke his apron strings', for the stones did appear to have been dumped from above rather than forced up from below.

The man-made object was a large wooden cabin set on the crest and facing south. It was not there for the magnificent view but to give a girl suffering from tuberculosis a chance to overcome that dread disease which haunted the lives of so many parents in those days and accounted for the deaths of a number of my friends. The fresh, clean mountain air was supposed to work wonders. I hope it did so for Miss Wallis whose parents had put themselves to so much trouble to provide a home for their daughter and themselves in that isolated spot, to which all food, fuel and drinking water had to be carried by hand or donkey cart.

On with quickening step to the edge of the escarpment with the town of Risca opening up below and the school, with its playing field, a green island in the rows of terraced streets. For a distance of about four miles the railway line between Cross Keys and Rogerstone would be within the range of my vision. It was not unusual to see as many as three coal-bearing trains in that short distance snaking their way slowly to Newport Docks, for this was the time of the First World War and Welsh steam coal was much in demand.

Then the steep descent through fields and into Mr. Harris's farmyard, where at that time of the morning his cows were gathered for milking, past the shunting engines of the Pontymister Steelworks, over the river, and in five minutes more I was at the school gates.

The walk was not my only exercise. In the lunch hour break I played football in the autumn and spring terms, becoming the school goalkeeper in my last year.

Occasionally in winter, football after school or detention for some misdemeanour involved a journey home in the dark but, knowing every yard of the ground, I had no fear of losing my way, even in fog, or

A section of the Mountain Path. Taken in 1980.

suffering harm from any cause. Crimes of violence (apart from fights arising from Saturday night drunkenness) were almost unknown in those parts then.

Snowstorms could be a minor hazard and I have not forgotten the occasion in March 1917 when, on my way home, I was faced at the summit by an intensely black sky and a gale force wind which drove sharp slivers of ice on to my face and hands, causing small cuts which bled. I was passing the area where outcrop coal had been worked many years earlier and the holes made by those excavations were close to the path. They were about twenty feet in diameter, and about fifteen feet deep with bracken-lined sides, and I took shelter in one of them until the ice-flakes gave place to snow-flakes, when I continued my journey, the gale force wind still making progress difficult even downhill. This was the notorious ice blizzard, long remembered for its ferocity and the fact that the snow and ice remained deep in some sheltered lanes for three months afterwards.

On all days in winter and many in summer, my mother saw to it that I wore or carried an overcoat, usually made of covert coating, cumbersome when dry and burdensome when wet. If light-weight, waterproof clothing existed, it did not come our way. This was not my only burden. Over my shoulder I slung a leather satchel carrying only as many books as I needed for that night's homework, and, on my way to school, my lunch which consisted most days of a few jam or paste sandwiches and, when available, a small round Welsh cake or two. This would now be regarded by many as an inadequate mid-day meal for a very active, growing boy but it was sufficient for my needs, if not for my appetite. Anyhow, it was wartime and food was scarce.

To that walk to and from school I have in recent years come to feel I owe at least as much of real value as the schooling that was its purpose. It gave me a well-developed physique (which has withstood much battering since) and a twice-daily exposure to the sights, sounds and scents of a naturally beautiful area and one endowed with monuments and marks of man's activity, ancient and modern. Yet if I were to tell the Gwent Education Authority (or any other) that less bussing and more walking to school might prove beneficial both to the children and the taxpayers the answer would be a rude one, with 'heartless reactionary' almost certainly a part of it. But I would not press the point. Our country lanes are no longer safe for children and not only because of motor traffic. I had the good fortune to go to school in a more civilized era.

19

The Grocer's Assistant

The class system that has dominated British society over the centuries and is now waning was still strong in 1916 when I did something which my parents felt was degrading and inconsistent with our social status: I became a part-time grocer's assistant and errand boy.

I was approaching fourteen years of age in the spring of that year, a pupil in a grammar school and, hearing that a shop in my home village of Machen in Gwent (we knew it as Monmouthshire) was temporarily without a boy assistant between the departure of one orphan from Dr. Barnardo's Orphanage and the advent of another in the autumn, I applied for the job and got it. So for weekends from after school on Fridays until about 9 p.m., and from 9 a.m. until about 11 p.m. on Saturdays, I stood in for a Barnardo boy. My pay was two shilling plus two free suppers and one free dinner.

I cherish the experience. To-day, I'm sure the laws of this land would forbid it—and much else that I enjoyed doing! I have often been reminded of those far-off days when now, deep in my retirement, I have accompanied my wife for a little household shopping and have recalled with wry amusement the contrast between the super-clean, super-efficient super-market and that rather dirty, fly-infested and untidy but most friendly village shop, as much a place of social intercourse and entertainment as of commerce.

Modern shopping, I find, seldom involves an excuse to speak or a need to be spoken to; even at the checkout desk it is easier for me to read the amount than hear it from the girl who, oftentimes, does not bother to look up—at least when she senses that a male customer is over seventy!

Not so at Meyrick's store. There, old and young were warmly welcomed: the old with sincere enquiries about their health, the young with a warm smile and often a joke. It was a place for talk, even at times of singing, a dispensary of news and gossip (it was there I first heard of the Battle of Jutland), a place where they also sold some necessities such as bacon and butter, sugars and spices, teas and tobaccos, bread and cheese, cakes and sweets, corn and meals and kerosene and candles: an amazing variety, especially as three other shops in the village stocked much the same commodities.

Poor old women came in for their meagre necessities, younger women for their family fodder, old men for their 'bacco' (usually Franklin's

Shag or Ringer's Shag—staggeringly pungent and foul smelling) and children for boiled sweets.

Serving a child with a ha'porth of sweets gave Ernest Meyrick a chance to perform a pantomime act. Taking a square of blueish paper (I can't remember why small paper bags were not provided) he would roll it into a perfect cone, pour in the bottled sweets and after weighing them carefully, often take one for himself, which he would toss to ceiling height and never fail to catch in his mouth. This feat always evoked admiration and, in me, emulation, but my failure rate was dishearteningly high and I consoled myself with the reflection that Ernest's mouth was at least twice as large as mine.

The name over the shop and on the billheads read James Meyrick and Sons, but James Meyrick and his wife had died some years earlier leaving the business to their two bachelor sons, Ernest and Alfred, and spinster daughter, Annie, who in 1916 were all middle-aged. I had been taught from an early age to call them Uncle Ernest, Uncle Alfred and Auntie Annie and did so believing that these were courtesy titles only. More than fifty years were to elapse before I discovered, in a belated enquiry concerning my ancestors, that they were indeed entitled to be so addressed, for Mrs. Meyrick had been my grandfather's sister and they were therefore first cousins to my father. The fact of this relationship, I now believe, softened somewhat my parents' opposition to my deputising for a Barnardo boy.

Alfred was morose and taciturn, seldom served in the shop and restricted his participation in the business to helping in the bakery and delivering by horse-drawn van the home-baked bread and consignments of provisions too heavy for me or outside the range of my deliveries. Annie, heavily built, physically inactive and wheezy with chronic bronchitis, served in the shop only when necessary and was usually to be found seated at the large kitchen table with daybook, large ledger and a pile of customers' account books in front of her and a large leather pouch, heavy with coins, slung round her waist, for she was the book-keeper and cashier. A fourth member of the household was Florence, a pleasant and hardworking cook and general servant who lived-in. When they had a Barnardo boy he, too, lived-in.

For a relatively small business the bookkeeping was immense, but that was the way things had been done for generations and the Meyricks were not the sort of people to institute change.

It was Unlce Ernest who was the life and soul of the business. I have said he had a large mouth; it was also loose lipped, producing a rich, deep voice that compelled attention, with a range from the mellifluous to the raucous as occasion demanded. When telling a story, and the business was seldom too urgent for that, with little encouragement, he would embark on a tale, and naturally employ the tones which the context called for, whether of comedy or tragedy, with the competence of a professional actor.

In those days, before modern medicine gave us an extended life-expectancy, deaths in the village, of both old and young, were heart-rendingly frequent and to hear Ernest describing the course of a fatal illness and ending with the words, 'and now he (or she) is DEAD' would send a shiver down my spine, such was his enunciation of that dread word. Naturally, it was always followed by a short silence.

Grocer by trade, actor by inclination and a talented singer withal! Some twentythree years earlier, that is in 1893, he had been a member of a famous Royal Welsh Male Choir that had gone to the U.S.A. to sing at the Great World's Fair held in Chicago, in celebration of the fourth centenary of the discovery of America by Columbus. They also gave concerts in other cities, both in the U.S.A. and Canada, and the triumphant tour (for it seems to have been nothing less) was followed by an invitation from Queen Victoria to sing before her at Windsor Castle, and there on the wall of the dining room behind the shop was a large photograph to prove it. It was an odd picture as it showed the large choir, rank above rank, all clothed in full evening dress with white ties, but unhatted, in the open air with the walls of Windsor Castle as background. Standing proudly among them, young, tall and good-looking—amazingly so to me seeing him daily a quarter of a century later—was Ernest. I often looked at the picture and wondered at the inscription, for Her Majesty had 'commanded' the choir to sing before her. I thought it should have read invited.

My intense interest in the U.S.A. and things American is in large measure attributable to Ernest's stories of his travels there as a member of the choir. They were many and varied and, told with his histrionic eloquence, could be heard time after time. Of his journeys on trans-continental trains, of receptions in magnificent hotels, of encounters with other Welshmen and of the rapturous reception given to the choir at its concerts and, especially, of a concert at Cleveland, Ohio.

There, said Ernest, in a huge audience, was John D. Rockefeller. Every item had been loudly applauded but, when the concert ended with the stirring 'Men of Harlech', John D. led the audience in a standing ovation which Ernest regarded as the highlight of the tour. (I thought fondly of Ernest when in Cleveland more than half a century later).

On Sundays, Ernest played the organ and led the singing in the Wesleyan Methodist chapel attended by my paternal grandfather and me until grandfather's death in 1911. If Annie, his sister, failed to attend through illness it did not much matter: Ernest was always able to tell her what the preacher had said and, with his gift of mimicry, how he had said it!

Of the business itself I have said little. It was more than a grocer's shop. They sold also fresh meat (bought from an abattoir), their own home-baked bread and buns and, from the granary adjoining the bakehouse, maize, wheat, and oats and the meals made therefrom: flour, bran, sharps, Indian meal as well as barley meal. The grains were sold to customers who kept chickens in their gardens or backyards (and many did so), and the meals to those who kept pigs, and it fell to me to do the weighing in relatively small quantities. We had no electricity or gas in our homes, so paraffin and candles were much in demand. I hated drawing paraffin by means of a built-in pump from a tank in the yard and pouring it into the customers' containers. I could not avoid getting the smelly stuff on to my hands and having to wash my hands thoroughly afterwards before attending to the further needs of the customer who might require fistfuls of biscuits out of a tin, as like almost everything else biscuits were not prepacked into the quantities desired by the buyers.

Almost everything was bought in bulk and the amount of time taken up in carving, cutting, scooping, weighing and wrapping was enormous, but the process was usually accompanied by Ernest

23

delivering his news and views on a variety of topics. Customers came prepared for a long wait.

Sometimes I was asked, when business by Machen standards was brisk, to weigh a pound or two of sugar, of which there were at least seven kinds—three or four browns and three or four whites—all in hessian sacks in the sugar room, on the gritty, sticky floor of which I hated to tread. The following procedure ensued: 1. place large square of blue wrapping paper on scales; 2. proceed to sugar room at rear of shop and, taking scoop, guess quantity required plus a little more; 3. weigh before intimidating eyes of customer; 4. return scoop and surplus to sack; 5. try wrapping the slippery stuff to form a neat, leak-proof package as demonstrated by Ernest; 6. this being wartime, take scissors and snip sugar coupon from customer's ration book.

On Maundy Thursday 1916, Ernest asked me to come in that evening to help him in the bakehouse where, in addition to the nightly bread-making, he had to make 'Hot Cross Buns.' Where Alfred was I can't remember. All I can remember is seeing Ernest, a Woodbine hanging from his lower lip, vigorously kneading and slapping a large amount of dough, the ash from the cigarette falling on to the dough wherein it rapidly disappeared from sight and might have contributed to the flavouring. (It had been rumoured in the village that a woman had complained to Ernest about a 'fag-end' in one of his loaves and, seeing Ernest at work, I was ready to believe it). Having rolled the dough to the thickness he wanted and added the currants and other dried fruits as well as spices according to the Meyrick recipe, he pressed out the bun-size discs and handed them to me for crossing. For this I used a tool like a small curry comb but instead of teeth it had two very thin pieces of sheet steel set to form a cross, and to make a cross that would be clearly seen after baking it was necessary, Ernest explained, to press it so hard as almost to sever the bun-to-be into four segments. It was hard work and I'm not surprised that other methods have been devised for forming a cross. Among my many unlikely jobs I can claim that once at least I was a Hot Cross Bun Marker!

The Shop Hours Acts came later, but in 1916 the shop remained open for as long as anybody wanted anything. After the last customer left on Saturday, by which time it would be approaching ten o'clock, Ernest, more often than not, asked me to help him with a little chaff-cutting for the van horse's Sunday sustenance. That horse must have had a voracious appetite. The amount of chaff I turned for while Ernest fed the machine seemed to me sufficient for seven horses for one day or one horse for seven days. So resolutely, if not very willingly, I turned the chaff-cutter after a day that had begun not less than thirteen hours earlier and sometimes about sixteen hours earlier. Then, arriving home long after my parents' bedtime, I was received, not with the appreciation I thought was properly due to me, but with a thundering row from my father. On my blaming my employer for my late return, he said, 'I'll have a word with Ernest about this,' but I don't think he did so.

The extra three-hour stint was when I had to take the horse to Caerphilly to be shod. There was a competent farrier at Lower Machen, less than two miles away, but I never asked why it was necessary to go to a smithy four miles away. One Friday night Ernest asked me, 'Can you ride a horse?' 'Yes,' I said truthfully: he had not asked what sort of horse. I had ridden cart horses bare-back and in cart harness as they ambled to and from the fields, but that had been the sum total of my equestrianism until that Friday night. On receiving his assurance Ernest went on to say, 'Well, I want you to take the horse to Caerphilly to-morrow morning to get him shod and I want you to be the first to get there as he must be back in time for the Saturday round.' This meant I had to be at the smithy before seven o'clock. So next morning, with only a snatched breakfast, I went to the stable, there to be confronted with a horse that, after taking one look at me, decided on a policy of non-co-operation. This was surprising as van horses generally, and this one in particular, had a reputation for being docile and tractable. When I approached the brute, bridle in hand, he sidled away, tossed his head, showed the whites of his eyes and kept his teeth so tightly clenched that I almost despaired of getting the bit between them. With that accomplished after a struggle, throwing a saddle over his back and tightening the girth was relatively easy. My next problem was how to mount him. I was thirteen and of medium height. As there was nothing near the stable on which to stand I led him to the low wall around the Church Hall on the main road. Placing a foot in a stirrup I flung myself across his back, whereupon he bolted, fortunately in the right direction. With arms around his neck I clung on while the brute showed a side of his character and a turn of speed that, so far as I knew, he had never before manifested. After about a mile, mostly uphill, he found the going hard and, becoming winded, decided on a change of gears—from gallop to canter, from canter to trot and from trot to walk, while we both got our breath back. I was now able to take hold of the reins and set my feet in the stirrups while congratulating myself on winning a battle of wills

25

and, so far as I knew, no one had witnessed my indignity—at 6.30 a.m. the road had been deserted.

Self-congratulation was short-lived. I heard and so did the horse, for he pricked his ears, a sound that heralded more trouble. Coming round the bend ahead was a horseless carriage and a big and noisy one at that. 'Jones's Modern Bakery, Caerphilly' had just acquired a motor van, a rare sight at Machen in those days. Whether that horse was as frightened by this mechanical monster as he appeared to be, or whether as a loyal member of the Van Horses Trade Union he felt that militant action was demanded of him against this innovation which he sensed would soon make him redundant, I don't know, but I can vouch for the vigour of his protest. His first move was to turn round and bolt back to Machen. This I checked by pulling mightily on the reins. On one side of the narrow road was the high stone wall of Gelli Wastad farmhouse and on the other the steep bank of the railway embankment. There followed a minor rodeo act in which the brute, frightened or angry or a bit of both, did his best to unseat me. There was no way past so the driver, a woman—for this was in the middle of the War—stopped and looked on with interest and, I'm sure, with not a little apprehension. After a struggle I was able to edge the horse past the van by keeping tight against the bank and, traffic-wise, on the wrong side of the road which was where we were when the driver first saw us. She now shouted at me, 'Where do you want to go?' 'Caerphilly,' I yelled back. 'Then get on the right side of the road!' In my headlong flight I had not given any thought to the rule of the road or it is possible that I had thought that equestrians, like pedestrians, could choose the side which best suited them.

We were early at the smithy, arriving even before the farrier and his helper, and so my horse was the first to be shod, but while he was being attended to others came and were tethered as those who had brought them, farmers and farmworkers, stood in a group chatting and laughing. I could have asked one of them to give me a 'leg-up' but preferred to use the mounting block. Then, as I was seating myself in the saddle and before I could get both feet in the stirrups, a lout among them used a heavy stick he was carrying to give my poor horse a resounding thwack across its rump. Never before had he suffered a greater shock and insult and his response was instant—to run away with me again. He could not have chosen a spot in Caerphilly better endowed with perilous possibilties. The smithy had been built against the outer wall of the ancient castle at the end of a narrow alley between two shops on the main road immediately opposite Pontygwindy Road, our route home. Where that alley joined the pavement on the main road was a spot where anyone emerging even with a walking horse should stop and look both ways. We came out of the alley and over the pavement and main road and into the Pontygwindy Road in a mad rush, mane, tail and stirrups flying and we were half-way to Bedwas before I gained some degree of control. Although the blacksmith's shop, the roadside shops and the alley have long since disappeared, I have seldom passed that spot since without reflecting how lucky I had been. An hour or so later the street would have been busy with people shopping and traffic, mostly horse-drawn it's true, but still lethal to a bolting horse.

Ernest was pleased to see us returning earlier than he expected. 'Good boy,' he said, 'I knew you could do it.' I did not feel called upon to tell him that it had not been too easy or that I would prefer to do my other work that day standing up—sitting down was much too painful.

Before the orphan lad from Dr. Barnardo's home came to take my place in the autumn I had two more rides to Caerphilly but I was now able to ride to the horse's rhythm and Prince and I had become good friends. When on the last occasion I went towards him bridle in hand I felt sure he gave me a knowing and friendly wink.

The author's paternal grandfather, Herbert Jones (1845-1911)

His paternal grandmother, Ann Jones, née Potter (1846-1936)

Siloam

Looking back, I have felt that what I saw and did as a boy might be of some interest to readers more than seventy years later who live in a very different world from the one I knew. Thus I have shown what working in a village grocer's shop involved and what work on a farm required of me. Another facet of my life, possibly an important one, concerns the effects on me of the religious influences to which I was much exposed, as I grew up under the shadow of, or in the light and warmth of—I offer a choice of phrase—Welsh Nonconformity at a time when it was a powerful force in the land, affecting the lives of everyone, adherents and the scornful alike. For example, the Nonconformists ensured that all inns were closed on Sundays and that in the villages, at least, no work was done or games played on the Sabbath.

What was the effect of such sunshine or shadow on me? I don't know. I can't imagine my life without its all encompassing aura of righteousness, or circumambient miasma of bigotry and hypocrisy (as some writers, Welsh ones included, have chosen to describe it). An attempt at assessment is clearly called for.

My first church-going (in our case really chapel-going) was when as a child of seven or eight I was taken by my paternal grandfather on Sunday mornings to the Wesleyan Methodist chapel at Machen. He was a keen member of that sect and held some sort of office in the church. In fact, he or my grandmother—I have never learned which—had inherited a treasured memento of John Wesley—some pieces of china which tradition claimed had been used by him when, in 1741, he had visited Machen and preached there. That precious china was kept in a corner cupboard in their little parlour and shown to visitors as a museum exhibit. (It is now in the possession of a cousin in the U.S.A.). I remember very little else of those early years but I enjoyed going to that chapel with him, my hand in his and clad in a sailor suit. It was a small chapel, cruciform in shape, and more like an Anglican church than a Welsh Nonconformist chapel. The people there were friendly, even jolly, a place of smiles, even laughter.

After chapel, Grandpa often said, 'Let's go and see old Mr. Newton.' There was also a Mrs. Newton but she didn't seem to count. Mr. Newton lived in a tiny cottage (part of a large house) opposite the chapel and was an army veteran, having fought more than fifty years earlier in the Crimean War as his medals above the mantelpiece testified. Grandpa took a kindly interest in everybody—old and young, chapel-goer or village drunkard—and was much respected, not only for what he was, a genuinely good man with a happy temperament, but also as manager of the local railway engineering works.

Mr. Newton died shortly afterwards and though I was only about eight at the time I have never forgotten his funeral because Grandpa, having notified the old soldier's former regiment of his death, a contingent consisting of about a dozen men was sent to carry the old veteran to his grave in St. John's churchyard. They were guardsmen with scarlet tunics, and tall bearskins: Machen has not seen a finer funeral since.

On Grandpa's death in 1911, I ceased to be a Methodist and became a Baptist, being sent on Sunday mornings to join my maternal grandmother, two aunts and the younger of my uncles in the family pew in Siloam Baptist Chapel, the larger of the two Baptist chapels in the village. My father claimed to be a Methodist but never went, so far as I can remember, to the Wesleyan chapel but used it as an excuse, I fear, for not going to the Baptist chapel more often than he could avoid doing so with my mother, my brothers and me, for the evening service.

> 'By cool Siloam's shady rill,
> How sweet the lily grows . . .'

Thus begins Bishop Heber's famous hymn but we must rid our minds of that image when considering Siloam chapel at Machen. Like the Siloam mentioned in the Bible, our Siloam had a pool, a boarded-over tank in front of the pulpit, in which those wishing to become members were baptized by immersion. Before the chapel was built (in 1837) the Baptists used the Rhymney river, a hundred yards away, but in my boyhood this was no 'shady rill' where sweet lilies grew but a noisome river, black with coal dust. Yet my friends and I bathed in it and survived. It is now running clean and clear again and the fish may return.

Siloam was a four-square building, with rectangular windows of clear glass (nothing Gothic about our Baptist chapels), a gallery on three sides, varnished pine seats throughout and on the white wall behind the large central pulpit in bold characters of blue and gold the words 'GOD IS LOVE.' Thus all was very plain and simple, yet not without some dignity and all expressive of the prophetic style of worship, without benefit (or otherwise) of ritual and ceremonial and typical of Welsh nonconformist worship throughout the nineteenth century and the early part of this one.

Sunday morning service began at 10.30 and ended about noon. The evening service began at six o'clock and ran until about 7.30, when, for the members there was a 'Second Meeting' which once a month took the form of a Communion Service. The main evening service was a repeat of the morning one: hymn, readings from the Bible, another hymn, a long extempore prayer (almost a sermon addressed to God), another hymn, collection, a sermon lasting usually not less than half an hour, the closing hymn and 'the blessing.' The three other chapels in the village offered the same programme.

Now for an assessment of the influence on me of all this churchgoing —as for some years I went thrice on Sundays: in other words, what good did it do me? Surely, to hear the Bible read twice or thrice on a Sunday must be of benefit to anyone! I attribute much of what I remember of whole passages in the New Testament to those early years, when, perhaps, for most of the time I was only half listening. I was an inveterate day-dreamer, but I woke up for the hymns: I loved them, both for their music and their poetry. Take the hymn which begins:

> 'As pants the hart for cooling streams
> When heated in the chase,
> So longs my soul O God, for Thee,
> And Thy refreshing grace.'

The images these words evoked were wonderful to me and I still regard them as inspired (I know they are based on Psalm 42), though I can't imagine their having the same appeal for professional animal lovers.

As for the singing, this, too, was splendid, especially at the evening service, when the men in the choir in the gallery above, mostly miners and railwaymen, gave full voice to hymns popular at the time such as 'Jesu, Lover of my Soul,' sung to the tune 'Aberystwyth'. A special favourite was 'All hail the power of Jesus' name' sung to the tune Diadem, the voices harmonizing naturally. The announcement of that hymn sent shivers of pleasurable anticipation up and down my spine and I was left with a sense of elation afterwards. Our hymn singing therefore must be set firmly on the credit side of the account.

The long so-called extempore prayers I recall with embarrassment and distaste. They seldom expressed what I felt and, to use a Quaker phrase, they failed 'to speak to my condition' or of my condition. For one thing, we Nonconformists were disinclined to acknowledge, once we had been 'saved,' that we were sinners and preferred to confess only to 'shortcomings.' I knew myself to be rather more than a short-comer and there were many, including the village policeman, P.C. Powell, who would gladly have testified to the fact! When later I got to know the General Confession in the Book of Common Prayer of the Anglicans I said to myself 'That's more like it'. 'Erred and strayed from thy ways like lost sheep.' Having looked for lost sheep on the mountains with my farmer grandfather I realized how perfectly apt that phrase was. And 'followed too much the devices

and desires of our own hearts.' Exactly! And 'left undone those things which we ought to have done: and ... done those things which we ought not to have done.' All neatly summarized in a few marvellously inspired lines! For the longwinded and high-flown extempore prayers, therefore, a debit.

Of the hundreds of sermons I heard at Siloam nothing remains or remained in my head or heart two days after hearing the best of them. The fault, no doubt, was mine because there were some very gifted preachers visiting the chapel in those years. For the sermons, therefore, neither a debit nor a credit.

The services, it will be seen, were very much a one-man affair. Apart from the hymn singing there was no congregational participation. Occasionally, a Welsh-speaking preacher, having read the text of his sermon in English, would repeat it in Welsh, claiming that the Welsh version was the better one. This never failed to evoke a murmur of approval from those present who could speak Welsh, that is the old or very old.

Of the Sunday School at 2.30 I can only speak with disdain. The teaching was perfunctory by teachers obviously not interested in their subjects nor in their pupils. The hymns tended to be sentimental. Some were of questionable validity for small children while others, such as 'Jesus wants me for a sunbeam' were quite ridiculous from the lips of a tough twelve-year-old boy who was pulling the hair of the girl in front of him or otherwise misbehaving as all too often we boys were. The hymn books were left-overs from the Torrey and Alexander Mission of a few years earlier. The net result of this Sunday-schooling was for me a trivialisation of the wonders of God and a diminution of the glories of Christ and so calls for a heavy debit.

On Whit Sunday it was the turn of Siloam to have our Sunday School Anniversary Service for which the other three Nonconformist Sunday Schools closed for the day and all came together at Siloam for a service conducted by a guest preacher which attracted a number of adults. On Whit Sunday, 1914, when I was twelve, I attended as usual and sat with other boys in the back row of the gallery and, by chance, in front of a window.

After the hymn preceding the sermon I turned round and looked over the river to the Tredegar Estate woods and on to the road below hoping to see, perhaps, a cyclist or maybe a horse and trap: there were few motor cars in our valley in those days and we could be sure none would be passing on a Sunday. Earlier, I had caught glimpses through the east windows of Machen mountain, my favourite playground, and I longed to be in the open air and not in this hot and stuffy chapel on this glorious day in May. Absorbed in imagining what I could be doing outdoors at that moment, it was with some surprise that I became aware that the preacher had stopped preaching and in the silence all I could hear sounded like a mouse in the wainscot. At the same time the boy next to

me was elbowing me vigorously in the ribs. Curious and annoyed at the prodding, I turned round to find the tall and thin special preacher pointing an accusatory arm at me while snapping finger against thumb. Then in the tones of a judge passing sentence on a desperate criminal he declaimed: 'If that boy who did not hear my text because he was looking out of the window and when he gets home will not be able to tell his parents what my text was, will now pay attention, I will read it again.' It was a long text

and he had not gone far when he stopped in mid-sentence. Out of the corner of his eye he had caught sight of a friend of mine, seated at the far end of our row and at right angles to the preacher where he felt safe from detection, grinning happily and waving his hand at me, obviously deriving the greatest pleasure from my discomfiture. Turning sharply and pointing that long arm at my friend, the preacher rebuked him with no less asperity: 'And if that boy waving his hand to him does not pay attention, he, too, will not remember the text. I will start again.' Whereupon he read it for the third time. This boy's intervention, I felt, lessened my disgrace, as a disgrace shared is one halved. I did not mind much the delight of my friends—and the greater delight of my enemies—what hurt were the superior smiles of the girls in the gallery opposite. As for the thrice read text, I did not remember a word of it.

On the following Sunday, my brother, Gwyn, and I went 'up home'— that is to our maternal grandparents' farmhouse for dinner. Seated with us round the table were Dad and Mam (our grandparents), our two aunts and two uncles, these being home for the week-end. I sat next to Auntie Annie. When the meal was well under way I was horrified to hear her say, 'A funny thing happened last Sunday at the Sunday School Anniversary . . .' There followed a blow by blow account of what happened. She ended with, 'I thought I would die trying to stop laughing.' All agreed that it was indeed a very funny story and, being otherwise engaged, no one looked up and saw my guilt stricken face.

In 1921, in which year my family left Machen for Barry, and I returned there only for week-ends with my grandparents, Siloam's last minister began his ministry, which, although he was not young, continued for fifty-one years. He was the Rev. Daniel Hughes, 'The Sledge-hammer Parson.' In an earlier pastorate at Pontypool he had fallen out with his church officers and they had barred the chapel doors against him. Our Daniel accepted the challenge and, taking a sledge-hammer, gained entry for himself and his supporters. He was a rebel by temperament and conviction. He supplemented the poor pay from the chapel with an uncertain income from professional lecturing, for which he was famous over a wide area. He had the countenance, voice and histrionic gifts that, had he so chosen, would have ensured success as a Shakespearian actor. His rendering of Dicken's 'Christmas Carol' was superb. Almost as popular was his 'My Ten Days in Quod.' Early in his career, he had refused, while living in Liverpool, to pay his rates on the grounds that part thereof would be applied to the support of Roman Catholic Schools wherein, he alleged, children would be taught that he and his fellow Baptists were heretics. Failing, for a reason which I have forgotten, to distrain on his goods (perhaps he had none worth taking!), the magistrates sentenced him to ten days in Walton Gaol, an experience, which like that of George Borrow when imprisoned for distributing Bibles in Spain, he turned to advantage. In that lecture he described his reception at the prison along with others in that day's gaol delivery—drunks, thieves and other dejected law-breakers. Seated at a table checking off the names of the newcomers was a prison officer who, without looking up, bawled at each man in turn, 'NAME!' 'David Jones, Sir,' or 'Patrick Murphy, Sir,' murmured the cowed captives. When it came to Daniel's turn, 'NAME!' the answer he got was 'DANIEL HUGHES' bawled even louder, as Daniel had a powerful voice. Surprised, if not shaken, the warder looked up and recovering his composure said, 'Aah Daniel, you're in the lions' den now!' 'Yes,' retorted the minister, 'I've heard them snarling!'

He was not only a fearless religious rebel in the Welsh radical tradition, who won my admiration, but he was also a dedicated Labour politician. To him Socialism was Christianity in action but in this he offended some and won over others. Mam was among those who were offended and, sorrowfully, gave up attending. Later, she was thankful to discover that Dick Sheppard, preaching from St. Martin-in-the-Fields, in London was a better exponent and defender of the faith in which she had been reared as a Welsh Baptist than the new minister at the local chapel. Machen was, and I believe still is, in the constituency at present represented in Parliament by Neil Kinnock and it might be thought that this alliance of religion with socialism would be acceptable to most people there, but dissensions and desertions in the chapel continued throughout that very long ministry and, with his going, the chapel also died after almost 140 years and the place whereon it stood knows it no more. Of the four Nonconformist chapels that flourished in Machen when I was a boy, Siloam, Ebenezer (both Baptist), Adullam (Congregationalist) and the un-named Wesleyan Methodist, only one, Ebenezer, the smaller of the two Baptist, is left, although the area covered by the village—and presumably the number of inhabitants—has doubled.

With their disappearance has gone, too, the indigenous Welsh culture in which I was reared. After more than fifty years' residence in England, I realise how distinct and precious that culture was. It has been replaced by the 'pop' cult, spread internationally by radio and television. And I'm saddened by it.

Caerphilly Cheese—Caws Caerffili

My maternal grandparents' farm was situated less than two miles from my boyhood home and it was on the stone-flagged floor of its kitchen that I had taken my first uncertain steps. I spent many hours there, a place of wonders and dangers, especially the gander's beak and grandmother's bees.

Although my grandmother had been making Caerphilly cheese since before I was born, it was not until the summers of 1917 and 1918 that I watched and took note of the process and that casually—not intentionally. In view of the wartime scarcity of labour I had been asked to spend my holidays 'helping on the farm' and, occasionally, after a hot and arduous day in the harvest field, I found the cool dairy a place of rest and refreshment. In a few years, farmhouse cheese-making in Wales, at least in the Caerphilly area, would come to an end and what I was witnessing was the end of an era. For some years it was impossible to find any Caerphilly cheese and when it reappeared on cheese counters it was a factory made product but so far as I could tell none the worse for that, being indistinguishable in appearance, flavour, smell and texture from the farmhouse article I had known and liked as a boy.

The farm was situated on rising ground a few miles from Caerphilly, and its famous castle, with its leaning tower, could be seen from its fields.

The method of making cheese that I saw my grandmother follow had been learned from her mother and the tools used must have been inherited from her grandmother. The milk came from Shorthorns and Hereford-Shorthorn crosses, with sometimes a Welsh Black or two among them. It was brought in pails without delay and uncooled from the cowhouse to the farmhouse dairy and immediately poured through a cloth-lined strainer into a large bath.

The house had been built on the side of a hill facing south, with the back set well below ground level so that the turf of the rising field outside the north window of the dairy was almost on the same level as the windowsill. The east window gave on to the orchard but the branches of an old apple tree, heavy with leaf and fruit during my summer holidays, came so close to the window as to deny any view. The result of both aspects, with grass and leaf so close to the windows, was to give a soft, diffused, greenish light in the dairy. The very thick stone walls and the stone flagged floor, together with the fact that it was set below ground level, made it a room of sweet smelling coolness on the hottest day of summer and there, on many a warm evening, I would watch my grandmother making Caerphilly cheese.

As I have said, the milk was brought straight from the cows and before it had time to cool—this question of correct temperature was, I understood, of great consequence—my grandmother would pour a little Danish rennet from an earthenware bottle into the still warm milk. It was also important that the right amount of rennet should be used but long practice and a steady hand had enabled grandmother to gauge the quantity needed for the varying quantities of milk simply by 'eye measure' as she poured.

The large bath stood slightly tilted on a low bench and grandmother, seated beside it, would pass her right hand forwards through the milk in a slow paddling motion, her fingers extended and as wide apart as possible. Now would be the time for talk; enquiries about school, questions on the day's work in the harvest field and reminiscences of her girlhood, among them, and especially interesting to me, the adventures of her brothers, two of whom had left home for America, one to become a sheep farmer in Texas and the other a lumberjack, the latter achieved only after a shipwreck on the Welsh coast a day or two out of Cardiff, followed by a crestfallen return home, a welcome in the form of a thrashing—for he had run away from home—and a more successful escape later.

For what I thought was a long time there was no sign of the cheese to be. The paddling movement would continue slowly with no apparent result, but eventually small curds could be seen which soon came to resemble small icebergs in the sea of milk. At a point which experience had taught grandmother was the right moment she would declare the cheese ready. Buckets were placed below the bath, the whey poured and the curds left in a great upstanding heap, to be cut deeply criss-cross with a kinife, presumably to drain off more whey.

The curds were then put in a cheese cloth, further drained and placed, cloth and all, in a shallow wooden vat with a loose round lid. This lid stood poised on top of the curds, inches higher than the rim of the vat, which was carried very carefully to one of the presses. These presses were museum pieces. They were very old but still performed their function perfectly. Gallows-like in structure, the weight was provided by a large wooden box filled with flat stones taken off the farm, the box being hoisted within the gallows by means of ropes and pulleys on a wooden windlass. The windlass was worked by iron pegs thrust through holes in the drum, the box being held in the up position by one or two of the projecting pegs resting on the top crossbar. The box was very heavy and this seemed to be a precarious method of holding it up, but I never heard of its failing.

The bottom cheese having been removed and the fresh one put on top, the windlass was carefully released and the box lowered very slowly on to the pile of vats, causing the new cheese to discharge a further flood of whey, which coursed through small channels in the base of the press and into a pan beneath.

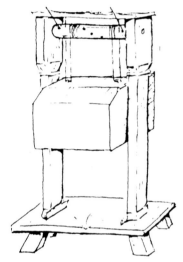

The cheese that had been taken from the press would be carefully examined and the rough edges, formed between lid and rim, trimmed off with a knife, to be eaten by me as they fell.

The last stage would be salting and removal to the cheese-room, another cool room but much drier than the dairy. Here the new cheese would join others on shelves to be turned daily until ripe. That was the Caerphilly cheese I knew and liked: made from fresh milk to which was added rennet and salt, but nothing else.

That wasn't the end. The whey was poured into large shallow pans, set on a big stone slab and kept there for several days during which a cream would form, to be skimmed off every morning until enough was collected to make butter in the hand-operated churn—a chore I would dodge if I could, although, as I was reminded, I was glad enough to eat the butter. Whey-cream butter, as we called it, was, I believe, an unusual product even in that district at that time. In these days I suppose it is quite unknown. What nourishment it provided I do not know and did not know and did not care. To me its nutty flavour was delicious and I would choose it in preference to 'shop' butter.

The skimmed whey was fed to the pigs who, too, were appreciative. In spite of some mild but well directed kicks it was difficult for me, a bucket of whey in each hand, to force a passage through their rugger scrums of welcome and much was spilled on my boots before I got to the troughs.

So the hay made milk, and the milk made cheese and whey, and the whey made butter and also fed the pigs whose bacon we had for breakfast. Subsistence farming! And my mother's generation would have none of it. The revolt commenced at the time of which I write, for my aunts were downright rebels. No cheesemaking for them, and hundreds of other farmhouse aunts were saying the same. 'Twice daily and seven days a week—not likely!' So during the nineteen-twenties the old presses went for firewood.

In the farmhouse we had that cheese for supper, along with the home-made bread baked in the brick-lined wall oven, and whey cream butter, and, when old enough, cwrw (beer) from the cask in the cool dairy. Delicious!

That meal is still a favourite of mine. 'But what about cholesterol?' I have considered this alleged hazard but having outlived almost all my boyhood friends, I can see no good reason for giving up a food I enjoy in an attempt, almost certain to fail, to prolong my life by a questionable act of self-denial in my eating habits.

A Welsh Farmhouse Christmas

Nant-y-ceisiaid Farmhouse 1918

When I was very young, the Christmas season did not begin in mid-November as it does now, but only a week or so before Christmas day. Its approach was announced by child carollers:

> Christmas is a'coming, the goose is getting fat,
> Please to put a penny in the old man's hat;
> If you haven't got a penny, a ha'penny will do,
> If you haven't got a ha'penny, God bless you!

This jingle, chanted outside our cottage door, was the signal for paying up. If they got the penny they asked for they would be content: it was as much as they expected. Tuppence was riches.

It had been preceded by 'When shepherds watched' or 'Good King Wenceslas'—children believed in giving value for money in those days—and

> We wish you a Merry Christmas
> We wish you a Merry Christmas
> We wish you a Merry Christmas
> And a Happy New Year.

For my brothers and me these wishes were seldom fulfilled. Some Christmases were reasonably happy and some, especially later ones, bitterly disappointing. For this reason my attitude to Christmas has been wretchedly ambivalent. From the middle of November when nowadays the shops begin to put on their Christmas displays, and throughout the growing commercially-kindled frenzy in December, I

40

have to fight a tendency to gloom and depression. At such times, I will confess to a sneaking sympathy with Scrooge, who, to his cheerful nephew's 'A Merry Christmas, Uncle! God Save you!' responded with, 'Bah! Humbug!' And I ask myself, 'Why?' The answer must be in childhood experience. If I felt I was alone in this it would not be worth recalling, but I'm sure among my boyhood contemporaries (not many of whom, alas, have lived so long) a number feel likewise. It is a story of great expectations and crushing disappointment.

I think it was 1915 when our Christmases turned sour for me. I was thirteen years old. Until then I had been pleased with my presents, modest enough as they were. Then, following the outbreak of war in 1914, toys became scarce and costly. The nadir for me was reached when, having outgrown stocking-packed presents, my sole Christmas gift was a pair of slippers. My disappointment was not lessened on being told I needed them: a true present, I thought, was not what I needed but something I wanted. I certainly did not want a pair of carpet slippers. After that I got no more gifts in kind: just a shilling or so to go into Newport to choose a book to add to my library of two books: 'Uncle Tom's Cabin' and 'The Story of Johnny Bertram' (a boys' adventure tale), both birthday presents. In fairness to my parents, I was the eldest of four boys, and it being wartime, toys were difficult to find and expensive while in those terrible war years our parents had much else on their minds including the clothing and feeding of four very healthy boys.

The shilling or so for the book was supplemented by a shilling or so from each of my grandmothers. That, too, was understandable and we expected no more. Before the age of the motor car members of both sides of the family went shopping only for what they really needed— 'consumerism' as a hobby or recreation was more than half a century away. My paternal grandfather had died in 1911. In 1912 or 1913 I was asked to escort my grandmother on a shopping expedition to Newport, a train journey of eight miles. She was only sixty-six, yet I remember her as being almost terrified by the hazards of the journey: she had ventured out so little alone. Though she lived for another twenty-four years, mostly active ones, I think that was the last time she went shopping for things to wear.

My maternal grandmother, eight years younger, was more adventurous and probably left the farm on such a foray at least once a year till she was over seventy, which seemed at that time to be a great age. So to go shopping for Christmas presents for boys was to them unthinkable.

41

'Mam' and 'Dad', grandparents and author's mother aged two—taken in 1880

The record in the family for avoiding shops was held by my farming grandfather and not only shops but public houses and restaurants also. When his farming business took him to Newport or Caerphilly markets the only building he entered was his bank, Lloyd's Ariandy (Money house). He maintained this record of avoidance for at least the last twenty years of his life—he died when aged seventy-six. His clothes were bought for him. Still less could we expect a gift in kind from him, nor can I remember receiving at any time money from him, even when working on the farm. It is only in retrospect and when recalling my dealings with our own grandsons that my grandpa's reserve and reticence strike me as odd. What we grow up with we accept. He left all household and personal disbursements to grandmother except those calling for payment by cheque. He was not mean, but gentle and kind, especially with children and his farm animals. But his shyness amounted to an affliction, which even as a child I noted and wondered about, for he would go to great lengths to avoid contact with strangers and sometimes even friends. Many years after his death when talking about him with my mother she blamed his tendency to misanthropy on an unfortunate boyhood experience. His father had been a colliery proprietor who, for some years at least, had prospered and had tried to give his sons what he regarded as a good education. So my grandfather, born 1854, had been sent to Clifton College, founded only a few years earlier, there to be educated as an English gentleman. He would have done better had he been sent to Llandovery College or Christ College, Brecon, and retained his Welsh identity intact, for at Clifton, as a timid, slightly built Welsh boy, speaking English as a second language, he was bullied unmercifully and the resulting unhappiness, my mother thought, had marked him for life. He had never spoken to me of his past and I have accepted what my mother said as being probably true. So from him, nothing at Christmas or any other time except a feeling of warmth and affection, never expressed in word or gesture, but real enough to me nevertheless.

Our Christmas Day resembled every winter Sunday, except that, unlike on Sundays, we did not attend chapel, as in those days few Nonconformist chapels in our part of Wales held services on Christmas Day and Good Friday. The Puritan tradition remained among us for it is to that influence I attribute the absence of such observance.

The postman came later than usual with a few Christmas cards, but none for the children. People then posted their cards on Christmas Eve or perhaps a day or two earlier and amazingly they always arrived on or just before Christmas Day. Our stockings containing an orange or tangerine and a few cheap oddments had been opened before dawn and examined and at least partly eaten by candlelight. Our main present, if there was one, came at breakfast time. Apart from a sprig or two of holly over a picture there were no decorations: certainly no Christmas tree.

The main ritual of the day was our visit 'up home' for dinner and tea with 'Mam' and 'Dad'. 'Up home' was my mother's home and 'Mam' and 'Dad' her parents. They were also 'Mam' and 'Dad' to their grandchildren.

Nantyceisiad farm was only a hilly mile or two away. There we were feasted every Christmas on a home-reared goose, with vegetables from their garden and a home-made Christmas pudding. In 1914 there were twelve of us: Mam and Dad, our two aunts, our two young uncles (Tom

43

a colliery surveyor at Ynyshir and Jack, a bank clerk), my mother and father, myself and three younger brothers.

After dinner, we boys, when we had toys, played with them; when without toys and the weather was not wet we played outdoors.

Tea at six o'clock was another substantial meal which never varied in what was put before us: home-baked bread, jam, a large apple tart, a custard tart and Welsh cakes made on a bakestone over the kitchen fire. I liked this meal better than the dinner. There were no decorations, not even a sprig of holly, yet there were many holly trees on the farm. Nor were any wine, spirits or beer served with, or after dinner, although a glass or two of 'cwrw' (beer) from the cask in the cool dairy would be available for the men at supper.

After tea, while the grown-ups sat and talked around the blazing log fire, over which hung a large picture of 'Cromwell refusing the Crown of England' (more evidence of the Puritan tradition), Gwyn and I played a card game or read by the light of the lamp on the dining room table and Vivian and Alan, much younger, either slept on the sofa or disported themselves with the sheep dogs on the rug in front of the fire.

About seven o'clock Dad, rising from his oak arm chair, would invite me to go with him to feed the cows. I was always happy to do so, taking pleasure in carrying the hurricane lantern and, going before him, opening the door on to the long passage in front of the manger and being greeted with the turned heads and luminous eyes of the expectant cows before Dad filled the manger with hay from the stack in the corner. Being sentimental, I would like to think he gave them extra measure for Christmas or a special helping of cattle cake. Only in retrospect have I seen that I was taking part in a Christmas scene: the winter night, the air frosty outside and warm and sweet in the cowshed, the manger with its hay, the straw covered floor and the placid animals. The image is strengthened as I recall Dad telling me that he sometimes found a tramp sleeping between the cows—a tramp who without money for a bed at an inn had sought the warmth of a cow's flanks rather than the company and cold of a vagrants' ward in the nearest workhouse.

They were Welsh cows, not so much by breed as they were mainly Shorthorns, but by understanding. Though Dad always spoke to me in English, when he had need to scold a cow he did so in Welsh and when in the spring and summer holidays I was sent to call them home for milking, I did as I had always heard him do, that is with as loud a voice as in those treble years I could command call to them, 'D-e-u-w-ch' drawing the sound out as long as my breath would allow. Had I instead yelled 'Come' I'm sure they would not have understood.

A less exciting Christmas for a child is hard to imagine but for me and the others it was always a day well spent. About nine o'clock we would leave, all six of us, for the downhill trudge to our own home, Dad, with his hurricane lantern, seeing us safely through the home field and across the plank bridge over the stream and through the strip of woodland to the stile in the hedge and the comparative safety of the stony lane.

That Christmas of 1914 was the last on which the whole family were able to get together. When the Christmas of 1915 came round both uncles, Tom and Jack, had joined the army although Tom, in a reserved occupation, could have claimed exemption. And Christmas 1916 must have been a desolate one for my grandparents, though as children we were not conscious of their sorrow, for Tom had been killed in the Battle of the Somme and Jack severely wounded in the same awful battle and still in hospital. My two aunts had also left home to be married: one to a clergyman and the other to a farmer and neither could get there for Christmas day.

Twenty-five years later and another war. Then for three Christmases the main blessing of Christmas for my wife and me and our two small

Thomas Arthur Thomas (Uncle Tom)

John Davies Thomas (Uncle Jack)

daughters was the confident belief that neither on the night of Christmas Eve nor on Christmas Day or the night following would we be bombed —we were living in a much bombed area in the South of England. But the same problem that defeated my parents during the earlier war now confronted us—presents for the children. Sweets were rationed, toys, except secondhand ones, almost non-existent.

For our Christmas night entertainment I read aloud from Dickens' 'Christmas Carol.' I enjoyed it: whether the two young girls did so I now doubt!

Shortly before my mother's death, aged one hundred and one, she said to me after a silence during which she had been thinking of the past, 'Did you know, Arthur, that your father hated Christmas?' I knew he never seemed to enjoy it—but hate it? I asked her why. 'He grieved that he could not give me and you boys the presents he wished to.' I was sadly shaken, my heart filled with pity and remorse that, as a child, I had looked for more than he could give. And he was no longer here so that I could tell him that it didn't really matter—we knew he was kind and willing.

The parents of to-day have an even tougher time: they have to contend with the pulling power of glamorized advertisements on television of toys and games at prices that many who watch them cannot, or ought not to, afford.

I was luckier that I knew at the time. The Incarnation is above all the feast of the family, when three or even four generations should find comfort and assurance in their coming together. I believe that grand-parents are important to young children and it is a pity that divorce and single-parent families are depriving many children of the affection at all times, and support in times of stress, of a grandpa and grandma. Indeed, that toyless, farmhouse Christmas was after all a privileged occasion, which many children, waist deep in toys, might well envy.

The Mowing Machine, the Flying Machine and the Gambo

I think I must have been among the first in these islands to see an aeroplane. The year was 1918, the place Nantygleisiad Farm, Machen, in Gwent, a hillside farm rented by my maternal grandfather from Viscount Tredegar. I was within a week or so of my sixteenth birthday, had just left Grammar School and, with my brother, Gwyn, then thirteen, had been asked to spend the summer holiday helping with the harvest on grandfather's farm, where because of the War, skilled help was difficult to obtain. Naturally, I put up a token resistance, games with friends offering a greater attraction, but we went, worked hard and benefited from the experience, but not much financially as if we were paid at all it would have been no more than a shilling or two at the end of the four or five weeks. But we lived on the farm and that in itself was a reward.

The day began as other days in that hot July had done. I had been awakened shortly after half-past six by the sound of my grandfather raking out the ashes from the previous day's kitchen fire, on which we depended for hot water and cooking. Experience had shown that further sleep was now impossible, however tired I might feel from the exertions in field and barn of the day before and, lying awake I waited for the other sounds of the new day. Our bedroom, Gwyn's and mine, that summer was in front of the farmhouse overlooking the farmyard. Through the low open casement window I could see across the wide valley to other farms, their fields dotted with cattle and sheep, and through the window came the scent of new mown hay mingled with that of roses, intensified by the heavy dew, from the tall bushes in the border below. Turning on my back, I would normally find something to interest me in the pictures on the rose-bud patterned walls or muse idly on the significance of the illuminated texts: 'THY WORD is a LAMP unto my feet, and a LIGHT unto my path,' 'So TEACH us to number our DAYS, that we may apply our HEARTS unto WISDOM.'

Suddenly, the early morning stillness was broken by the barking of the two sheep dogs and in my mind I saw them rushing from their kennels to welcome grandfather as he emerged to begin his outside duties of the day. First, to let out the geese from their noisome den, the gander hissing and the dogs barking in defiance but keeping a respectful distance from the gander's beak, followed by the release of the chickens, cackling and chuckling as they scrambled to get through the small hole in their fox-proof stone house, which they had entered so sedately at dusk the previous evening. The barking dogs had aroused the pigs, now squealing and grunting in anticipation of their breakfast, as well as a calf calling plaintively for its mother in the cowshed next door, whose lowing response added to the farmyard cacophony. In a minute or so the excitement would be over and soon I could count on hearing sounds indicating that grandmother was preparing breakfast in the kitchen. I knew what next to expect: 'Arthur, Gwyn get up!' from the foot of the winding stairs. 'All right Mam,' from me. Gwyn slept on, tired out. I, too, was a sluggard even when a few minutes later the call was repeated, this time with a degree of asperity. But unknown to her, Mam—by the way, we knew our maternal grandparents, Welsh fashion, as Mam and Dad, by which names also they were known to their own children—in

leaving open the door at the foot of the stairs had allowed an ally to creep up the stairs and into our room. This was the smell of our home-produced bacon cooking in a Dutch oven before the now blazing fire. Hanging from hooks, the very fat rashers oozing melted fat on eggs sizzling in the tray beneath, gave off a smell

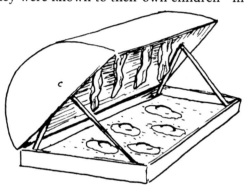

that I found irresistible. Nothing could have been more effective in getting me out of bed. Eaten with Mam's home-baked bread, the bacon and eggs made a perfect breakfast—perfect in terms of enjoyment, of course. From a health standpoint, such a meal is now regarded as almost lethal, but in my 83rd year I'm glad that 65 years ago there was no one to tell me that I was slowly killing myself.

Breakfast over, Gwyn and I shared the first duties of the day: to feed the chikens, pigs and calves, carry milk from cowhouse to dairy, and water in cans from the spring in the wood at the bottom of the home field, all water for drinking and cooking being so obtained. A word about that water: it was clear, cool and if not delicious at least refreshing and often on a hot day, disdaining the slightly warmed and stale water in the cans, I took a cup to the tap which controlled the impounded spring just as modern boys, sons of moneyed parents, go to the 'fridge for a can of Coca-cola.

To get to the spring I had to cross a stream. From this stream the farm derives its name, Nantygleisiad or Nantyceisiad, which I understand means the brook of the salmon-trout, much too grand a name really, as all Gwyn and I caught in it were eels and they were too small to eat.

If the sheep had not been looked at the day before a round-up was called for, so that Dad could inspect them for signs of fly-strike or footrot. For the former, I carried shears and a tin of Stockholm tar; for the latter Dad used his sharp pocket knife.

By now it was getting on for ten o'clock and time to continue mowing the Long Field, begun the previous day. So with the two horses, Dad, Gwyn and I went to the half-mown field where the old and heavy Bamford mower awaited us, the dew-soaked grass having sufficiently dried out to allow mowing to be resumed.

The crop was particularly lush that July and Gwyn and I were set at opposite ends of the field to rake away at two corners the last swath to allow the knife to make an unimpeded entry to the next round. The day was hot, the work easy, so leaning on my rake, I had time between rounds to look about me. Why that scene remains so vividly in my mental picture gallery I can't explain: it might be due to what was about to happen. I had worked in hayfields before and would do so later, but as Wordsworth with his 'inward eye' beheld the 'host of golden daffodils' so that scene of bucolic peace has never been effaced from my memory. The tall standing grass, rippling in the light breeze, presented a picture of sublime loveliness to the eye, while the freshly mown grass and a myriad of flowers gave off a fragrance that even a country lad could not ignore. It was natural meadowland, the field, at least within living memory, having never been ploughed.

I have spoken of grass and the field did contain a variety of grasses, prominent among them the quaking grass known to us children as 'shivery shakes,' but what impressed me, a strong, healthy, sun-tanned sixteen-year-old on that July morning was the colour provided by the many flowers which flourished among the grasses. To an agronomist this high flower content might indicate a crop of poor nutritional value, but I'm writing about beauty, not economics. Large 'dog-daisies,' a sprinkling of red poppies, the mauve scabious, the blue cornflowers, the red and yellow vetches, the bright buttercups and the red and white blossomed clovers in which Mam's bees were busy and, flitting over all, butterflies of various colours, now, alas, seldom seen as herbicides, insecticides and pesticides have fulfilled their deadly but presumably necessary purpose.

49

In the background as I faced the standing grass was Mynydd Machen, its lower slopes covered with bracken. Below me, the wide expanse of the valley, with other woods and farms belonging to Lord Tredegar and, in the foreground, beyond another of Dad's fields, the hamlet of White Hart with its few cottages and two pubs, and the Brecon and Merthyr Railway constructed by my paternal great-grandfather, a Civil Engineer, some fifty years earlier, inconveniently tight against them. In 1918 it was a busy line with train after train loaded with coal descending slowly to Newport Docks, interspersed with passenger trains, one about 12.30 taken by us as our dinner bell as we carried no watches. About every two hours a train, owned by the Alexandra Docks and Railway Company passed on its way between Machen and Pontypridd via Caerphilly. This train consisted of a small engine and two coaches only, but they were strange ones. They were long and had straw pleated seating ranged down the sides with a wide central passage, and at the ends they had open observation platforms on which I loved to ride. Some years later I recognised them in Wild West films and, later still, I learned that they had been brought to this country by Barnum and Bailey's Circus and left behind when the circus returned to the U.S.A.

Dad had made several circuits and the island of standing grass was very narrow when I heard a strange sound. Mechanical, not natural. Something wrong with the mower, I thought, which was closely approaching, the horses, their heads nodding and their shoulders wet with sweat, pulling hard. But Dad was sitting unconcerned and if any defect was developing he would be the first to hear it, being more an engineer than a farmer. I then realised that this noise was coming from above. Until then the only common sounds from above were the song of skylarks, the cawing of crows and the crack or rumble of thunder. Turning sharply I saw with amazement my first flying machine, a biplane, with only a pilot in it, his helmeted head clearly visible as he dipped his wings from side to side as if wishing to take in all that was happening below. He certainly got some fun out of seeing me if, as is more than likely, flying slowly and, according to modern rules, illegally low, he saw me waving both arms and yelling as I tried to attract Dad's attention. Dad had come to the end of the cut but the noise from gears and cutting bar had prevented him from hearing the aeroplane. Now, in turning, he caught sight of my demented antics and 'Whoa'd' the horses to a stop as he shouted 'What's the matter?' 'A flying machine' I yelled, pointing to the sky above his head. Risking toppling over backwards but with the sun in his eyes he failed to see it, although the chatter of its engine indicated that it was very close. Defeated, he turned to me again. 'Where is the bugger?' 'Above you, Dad.' By this time the flying machine was sufficiently in front of him as to provide a breath-taking view of this marvellous object, a harbinger of wonderful things to come.

That day was a memorable one for me as this blow-by-blow account of it is proof. Not only had I heard and seen a flying machine passing close to me, I had heard for the first time in my sixteen years a forbidden word pass Dad's lips. It was the measure of his excitement, and the shock of hearing him swear for the first time was almost as profound as the impact upon me of the flying machine. He was a shy and reserved man, whose restrained conversation never exploded into oaths or cuss words even under the greatest provocation, and I'm sorry to think that he frequently had cause to be angry with Gwyn and me as we damaged or lost his carefully preserved tools or otherwise misbehaved. Mam, on the other hand, placid and serene both by nature and in pursuance of her deeply held religious faith, often told us in righteous anger what she thought of us and when her English failed to express fully her degree of exasperation would revert to Welsh, which we only vaguely understood but we got the message.

We talked of little else that day as Dad, using the horse rake, formed the teddered hay of an earlier mowing into windrows which Gwyn and I converted into haycocks ready for Edward Thomas, who, having snatched a hasty tea after a full day's work as a roadman, would come on the morrow to help pitch. He lived in the white-washed cottage in the lane below. He pitched on one side of the gambo, usually taking cleanly the whole of a haycock on to his fork and, lifting it effortlessly, deposited it carefully on the gambo where Dad was forming what he hoped would be a well balanced and cohesive load. I, on the other side, straining to emulate Edward's performance and never succeeding, had to make two assaults on every haycock and then often leaving some hay for Gwyn to rake to the next one. That, too, is a scene I have not forgotten. While the war in France was still continuing in all its fury it was a picture of peace. Dad and Edward Thomas, in tones of equality, spoke to each other as the work went on, Gwyn and I understanding only a little of it as they conversed in Welsh. Their talk, it was plain to us, was about matters serious—the war, about those in the village who had been killed, wounded or gone missing, about other farms and farmers and farm crops, that is about things that matter to country folk, with never a joke or a laugh. Edward Thomas was tall and fully bearded with a suggestion about him of solidity, cleanliness and strength. I though he was old but now believe he was under fifty.

I have mentioned 'tones of equality' in their conversation as if that were a fact worthy of special notice. It was. Between the farmer and the labouring man there was a social gap which neither recognized, but each acknowledged the other's worth. This was a factor in Welsh rural life of which I became aware only after living for some time in an agricultural community in the south of England, where grades of social difference were clearly defined by deference on the part of farmworkers and woodmen, and a patronising posture on the part of their bosses. In rural Wales where the farmworker or blacksmith might well be a poet or composer and, more often than not, was thoughtful and serious, imbued with a respect for the things in life that really mattered, there was not that social distinction when I was young. I recall the respectful tones in which Mam spoke to, and of, Mr. (always Mister) Davies, a humble cobbler, with a knowledge of the Bible that perhaps almost equalled her own.

One other observation: they spoke in Welsh. That was 1918. Writing in 1955 the Rector of Machen, recalling the consecration of St. John's Church a century earlier, mentioned that the sermon at the evening service on that occasion had been in Welsh and added that 'to-day there is not a single native of Machen who can speak Welsh.' Gwyn and I were natives of Machen and Gwyn had a fair smattering of Welsh, but never spoke it except for an odd phrase or two. You might well wonder why, when we were taught Welsh at school and heard it daily in the farmhouse for weeks on end where Dad and Mam spoke to each other only in Welsh, we were not encouraged to learn it. The point was never raised. I can only suppose that they knew we were destined to make our way in an English speaking world where, they assumed, Welsh would be of no use to us and the sooner we spoke good English the better it would be for us. Sometimes they had difficulty in translating Welsh words and idiom into English.

I have also spoken of a gambo. Nowadays, many in Wales have never seen a gambo and in England the word is unknown, yet when I was a boy almost every Welsh hill farm had a gambo. Made by village carpenters and blacksmiths, it was a simple form of open cart very suitable for hillside conditions, consisting of a strong wooden platform slung over a pair of wheels, with a rustic pole wedged into a hole at each of the four corners and a rail above each wheel, thus making it easier to contain hay and straw and bracken (then often used as bedding for animals when straw was not readily available).

That scene in the hayfield almost seventy years ago provides a basis for assessing change. The gambo went for firewood soon afterwards and few children in Wales to-day have known the pleasure of riding on one. Nor are children now needed or even welcomed in the harvest fields where fast moving machinery is an ever present threat to life and limb. Two men, with tractor and tractor-mounted or towed implements, can do all the work quickly and competently.

Horses, too, have been degraded: never now dignified by honest work but demeaned by being merely playthings, but better such than that the noblest of animals should vanish from our country lanes, hunting fields and racecourses.

And when I saw that little hedge-hopping flying machine, not even in my wildest flights of fantasy (and as an inveterate day dreamer I was not

53

lacking in imagination) could I have forseen the day when, with some hundreds of others, I would travel across the Atlantic, apprehensively and uncomfortably, in the belly of a Boeing.

I'm glad I was born in 1902, to have ridden on a gambo, worked in hayfields and cornfields and shepherded sheep, to have ridden on the 'Wild West' train to Caerphilly and travelled in ships. As for this last pleasure, which increasingly is becoming a luxury, what landing by air can compare with that arrival in Helsinki's beautiful harbour on a sunny June morning to the strains of the ship's band playing Sibelius's 'Finlandia!' But that experience was some fifty years later and outside the scope of these tales.

Part II

Yes, I was a Yesman
1918 - 1923

Of Shoes—and Ships—and Sealing Wax

In July 1918, almost on my sixteenth birthday, I left Pontywaun
County School, Risca, and a few weeks later received a certificate which
showed that I had done moderately well in an examination roughly
equivalent to the later 'O' level. This led me to believe that I had been
educated. Experience, mostly painful, was to reveal how little I knew
about anything and anybody, including myself. I had wanted to become
a sailor, an idea which appalled my parents, who were only too conscious
of the deaths at sea of many of their friends and acquaintances serving in
Cardiff-owned steamers. They insisted on my becoming a clerk: any
sort of clerkship would do. Working conditions were usually clean and
the calling a respectable one. Living in a coal-mining area I might have
become a colliery clerk but for the fact that I had an uncle, vicar of a
parish, who had a rich shipowner as a church-warden and, thanks to a
word in the ear of that important man, I was granted an interview with
the company secretary. My parents were delighted at the prospect of my
becoming a junior clerk at Cardiff Docks—that mecca for so many who
aspired to make money. Perhaps, in time, I would become a millionaire
myself! Others who had begun as clerks had done so.

The interview was conducted in the deeply carpeted boardroom
across a long leather covered table, and what with the magnificence of
these surroundings and the gravity and dignity of my questioner, I was
overawed and answered hesitantly and nervously. I came away feeling
sure I had failed. There was Mr. William P. Annear, tall, handsome,
white-haired with a trim French beard and a waxed moustache to
match, sartorially, perfectly turned out according to male fashions of
that time; and there was I, a young, ill-educated rustic in a shabby suit,
red of cheek, with hands so roughened and stiff from farm-work that
they could hardly hold the pen I was given for a test of my competence
as a shorthand writer. My speech too was no help. Even Cardiffians,
with a sniff of superiority, would insult me with 'You come from the
valleys!' With these drawbacks it seemed impossible that I should ever
be allowed to set foot on the first rung of the ladder to fame and fortune.
I was told to wait for a vacancy but if anything else should come my way
I would do well to take it. I waited, but not in idleness. My farmer
grandfather at Machen and a farmer uncle at Rhiwderin found me
useful with so many men away in the war and I returned to the harvest
field from which I had departed for the interview.

Haymaking was followed by the corn harvest, then the mangold pulling, potato bagging in the field, my boots heavy with clay, and, worst job of all, picking brussels sprouts, an agonisingly painful task on frosty mornings, when blowing on frozen fingers availed not at all. When it rained I wore a hooded sack over head and shoulders.

It was from such work and this rustic environment that late in October, when I had almost given up hope of escape from this sort of life, I received a letter requiring me to present myself at the company's offices on Monday, 4th November, at 9 a.m. ready to begin work in the secretary's department for a probationary period of three months at a wage of five shillings per week. As Cardiff was not at that time within easy daily reach of my valley home at Machen, this meant going into lodgings. It also meant that, with a wage of less than a shilling a day (for we worked until mid-day on Saturdays), I was a continuing expense to my parents who had three younger sons to support.

I had been at work a few weeks, or rather learning to work, for my duties were all strange to me, when I learned without doubt that I was there on trial. My duties included typing from drafts penned by the secretary, some shorthand-typing (the chief kindly reducing the speed of his dictation to my poor shorthand speed as, with fingers made clumsy by farm work, I tried desperately to keep up with him), copying letters in the copying press and filing letters inwards in 'lever' files. I shared these duties with another boy who had been there almost a year and we were told that when my three months were up one of us would have to go, for the Armistice had been signed and those former employees who had survived the War would be returning. It was he who had to go and he did so gladly; both the decision and his cheerful acceptance of it surprised me greatly. He had had a longer and better training and I still felt quite unfitted for the job, and, as other members of the staff said later, looked it. My weather beaten countenance and hands coarsened by hard manual work, together with my unfashionable country clothes and boots, suggested the plough-boy. True, I was without straws in the hair, but my head carried something much worse, a ringworm infection, of which I was very conscious and did my best to hide. A bald patch about the size of a penny on the side of my head had been caused by my neglecting to use the customary greasy, tweed cap worn reversed by all milkers at that time, men and women alike, and I had rested my unprotected head against an infested cow's flanks.

Howard Spring, novelist and journalist, had been an office boy in an accountant's office at Cardiff Docks about seventeen years earlier. Reading his autobiography I am struck by how little things had changed between the turn of the century and the end of the 1914-18 War. We had a number of experiences in common. We both worked under the close supervision of members of the Plymouth Brethren sect: his boss was a Public Accountant, mine was a Chartered Secretary, and we each received gifts of clothing from them. Howard Spring had been given a tie as his boss could not stand the sight of the boy's Eton collar stud; mine shuddered at the sight of my boldly striped shirts (discarded by a well-to-do American cousin) which the heat in the unventilated back room in which I had to work forced me to display on hot summer days. Acknowledging my poverty and being too kind to make a disparaging comment, Mr. Annear turned to me one morning with the instruction, 'Go round to Edward Roberts's and get an office jacket for yourself and tell them to charge it to my account!' I did so gratefully and wore the light grey, unlined cotton jacket every summer for some years. Howard Spring showed a more spirited reaction: he wore the tie only until he could afford to buy one and threw away the gift one—not because he didn't like it but because of the insulting manner of its presentation: 'Here boy! Take this, and wear it!'

In 'And Another Thing' Howard Spring said of the members of the congregation who attended Conway Road Wesleyan Methodist Church, to which he went in his teens, that they 'were, almost to a man, good, safe, well-to-do commercial people. Devon and Cornish names were common among them, for though Cardiff is in South Wales it is not of South Wales. The great names in the commercial life of the town were not, in the main Welsh. Cornwall and Devonshire, offering small chance to those of their sons who did not take to the sea or the land, exploded across the narrow water of the Bristol Channel. The Welsh in the 'hills' were the labourers: the invaders, for the most part, filled the commercial and professional offices.' This was so in 1918, although by then the Welsh were beginning to realise that they were missing something by entering exclusively the teaching and preaching professions and there were now some Welsh managers, accountants and lawyers in and around the Coal and Shipping Exchange. That business world however was still dominated by men who, if they had not been born in Devon or Cornwall, were the sons of parents who had.

Thus it was in a family firm of shipowners, founded in Cornwall in the middle of the nineteenth century and transferred to Cardiff some years later, that I now found myself set on the lowest rung of the professional ladder, being solemnly told that if I showed myself to be diligent and trustworthy I would be instructed in the ways of commerce and trained to become an efficient company secretary and private secretary.

The two principal directors, sons of the founder, had been born in Cornwall and had come over to Cardiff with the family and family possessions in one of the two sailing ships which constituted the whole fleet at that time. Soon they went over to steamships and over the years they added coal exporting and iron ore importing to their shipping business as the main activities of the many companies then in their ownership. In addition, they held controlling interests in companies offering ancillary services to shipping, such as shipstore merchants, ship provision merchants and ship-repairers, which they also managed. To all these companies, Mr. Annear acted as secretary. He also served the two principal directors as their private secretary. He, too, was a Cornishman as was also the Marine Superintendent, Captain Hodge, who had served in sailing ships and whose loud but not unpleasant West Country voice suggested that he would be more at home on an open bridge deck than in the confines of a city office.

The business had prospered and twenty years before my joining the firm had developed sufficiently to justify the erection of what was then regarded as a prestigious office block for sole occupation. Internally, the accommodation ranged from the luxuriously appointed boardroom to the dark and airless dungeon in which I had to work. The secretary's office was next to the boardroom and behind the secretary's office was the said dungeon enclosed in floor-to-ceiling partitions, half-glazed in Muranese glass on three sides, with a solid wall on the fourth side. In front, therefore, the secretary's office, on two sides a dark, windowless and airless passage and on the fourth side a windowless wall. This meant that, except on sunny mornings when the east-facing secretary's office collected enough light to allow a little of it to filter through the Muranese glass partition, we had to work by the light of two low-wattage bulbs slung low over the desks. That was not so bad. What was bad was the absence of any ventilation apart from that which came through open doors and internal fanlights. These were of little use as they either communicated with a room in which the windows were seldom opened (when an east wind blew, coal dust from the tipping at the docks was a problem), or with a dark corridor which served as an excellent funnel for coke fumes from the boilers in the basement.

By diligence and good luck I had survived the three months' probation, but I learned much later and indirectly, that my chances of surviving physically had been rated as pretty poor. My months of farmwork had been preceded by three years wherein my daily walk to and from school had involved the ascent and descent of a mountain over a distance of about three and a half miles, and my complexion, chest and limbs testified to the value of this necessity—a privilege denied to the car-borne kids of fifty years later. But in a couple of months in this den the ruddy cheeked boy had become deathly pale and hollow cheeked and my kind boss feared (and privately communicated his fears to my family) that I was, or soon would be, developing consumption, which was very prevalent and a killer in those days. I had not been there more than a few months before a colleague of my own age succumbed to it and died within weeks of its apparent onset, and another was known to be suffering from the disease. A millionaire's office with working conditions for the junior staff that would not be tolerated to-day! Only in looking back do I realise what little thought was given in those days to measures for reducing health risks in factories and offices. The general attitude seems to have been one of fatalism: if we got TB or any other disease it was just bad luck.

In addition to the unhealthy working conditions, I also suffered poor living conditions; for some months in 1919 I was in lodgings with other boys and men, where the landlady, defeated by the continuing wartime food rationing and the scarcity of off-ration foods, refused to provide more for us than the rationed foods which she bought on our behalf. These quickly ran out and lacking meat, eggs and fish, it was a problem to find something to eat. On several occasions my main meal of the day consisted of dried peas, boiled without any meaty or fatty additive, and served with melted cocoa butter which was supplied in place of margarine when that commodity was scarce. This, for a lad of seventeen was quite inadequate and I am now never surprised to learn, having survived myself, how little one can eat and yet exist, even actively, at least for a time.

Those Put In Authority Over Us

The two principal directors were in their sixties. The senior brother, chairman of all the companies in the group, was at that time also chairman of the Coal and Shipping Exchange and very likely the most influential business man at Cardiff Docks. The younger brother was

Member of Parliament for Cardiff South, the constituency represented later by a future Prime Minister, James Callaghan. The four junior directors were their sons, two from each branch of the family.

Although more than sixty-five years have passed since I joined their staff and more than sixty since I left, I will not name these men, but refer to them as the Chairman and the Member. In this way I hope to reduce, if not wholly avoid, the risk of hurting the feelings of any grandchildren or great-grandchildren who, identifying these men, may be hearing for the first time that not all who served these ancestors of theirs held them in high esteem, notwithstanding the honours and respect accorded them by the powers that be from the Crown downwards.

They were not dishonourable men and, although they paid me hardly more than a pittance, they treated me fairly according to the standards at that time in that community. It is only by the standards of to-day that they seem to be less than praiseworthy.

Their private secretary and secretary to the many companies they owned or controlled, self-effacing and reticent in his lifetime, was in truth a noble man. William P. Annear, a founder member of the Chartered Institute of Secretaries, was a man of whom his descendants can be proud, for in all his ways he sought excellence and achieved it without any loss of integrity, generosity and compassion.

The Chairman with his bearded head, stocky figure and portly stance bore a striking resemblance to King Edward VII, who had died eight years earlier but whose picture, with that of Queen Victoria, still hung on many a cottage wall. I assumed that as a Wesleyan Methodist his resemblance to the late king was restricted to appearance: it was with surprise that I learned some years later that his tastes and manner of life, at least in private, were also akin to those of his late majesty.

Naturally his style of dress was also Edwardian; never without a waistcoat, sometimes white or cream, and never without a massive gold watch chain. And almost always, summer and winter, with light grey or fawn spats over his boots. Whether because of his great wealth or his unrelenting sternness or the deference accorded to him by other men, I stood in dread of him even when I discovered that under his stylish and expensive clothing he was not so very different from me after all! When my presence was required in the boardroom I was usually summoned by the Chairman or his brother banging a bell but sometimes, especially if I had blundered in some way, I would be shouted for. Once, a louder shout than usual sent me into the boardroom with knees knocking to discover the Chairman clutching one of his knees in apparent agony. On raising his trouser leg a large darning needle was seen to be harpooned into the knee-cap. I was relieved to find that this was something for which I could not be blamed and was surprised by the revelation that a man so rich bothered to have his woollen underclothes darned (I have since wondered how it came about that the stabbing had been so long delayed for he had travelled by train and had been in the office an hour or more before the needle struck. I never heard what fate befell the sewing maid). This man, in spite of his leading position in the commercial life of Cardiff at the time when the city reached its zenith, never won my liking or respect.

His brother, the Member, was a continuing source of wonder to me. From the beginning he seemed to me to be overdressed, over bejewelled (he wore large gold rings and, until it was pinched, a huge pearl tiepin, as well as a showy gold watch chain) and his blustering manner was made more offensive by a guttural enunciation when speaking, due to a speech impediment. I owed my introduction to the firm to this man and never forgot the fact but took an instant and growing dislike to his podgy appearance and pompous manner. However, Mr. Annear, his private secretary (and my boss) never failed to show a dutiful respect to him which I'm sure he could never have felt, for he was no fool when it came to weighing up men—and boys! He thus taught me to be respectfully obedient to those set in authority over us, whether we esteem or detest them—which was no bad thing, especially for one destined to become a private secretary!

Both men were regular churchgoers: both had been Methodists but the Member had forsaken Methodism for the Church of England. Both gave largely and ostentatiously to charity, the M.P. declaring that he took for himself no part of his parliamentary salary of £400 a year, but donated half to the Royal Infirmary, Cardiff and half to the Royal Hamadryad Seamen's Hospital. I suppose this beneficence was worth a few hundred votes!

I have never ceased to wonder how a man possessing few basic qualifications—a fine appearance, education and intelligence—and such obvious disadvantages (as a public speaker he was hardly intelligible, and, when understood, boring) could win an election. He got into Parliament in the first place unopposed. Due to the stress of the 1914-18 War, when the seat became vacant, an election was held to be unwarranted and the seat went to him as chairman of the local Conservative Association. However, he held it in two General Elections. What also strikes me as extraordinary is the fact that all three Cardiff seats were held simultaneously by shipowners, two on behalf of the Conservatives and one for the Liberals, and of the three only the Liberal, Sir William Seager, had the character and qualities to justify his choice as candidate and his success at the polls. And this in a predominantly working-class city! I thus learned that ambition, backed by dogged determination, and supported by bluff and money (and undiscriminating Trade Union loyalty) can propel one a long way along the road to Westminster. Nowadays, the Member would never have got on to an approved list of candidates. Instinctively, I disliked and distrusted him but I had no standards by which to judge him and assumed that the electors of South Cardiff were better able to assess his qualities than I was. Blundering in wonderment from one strange encounter to the next I accepted other people's ideas about their own importance, and was unable to distinguish between the meritorious and the meretricious. I distrusted that which I felt instinctively—although it would have been a better guide.

But I was learning quickly and in the General Election campaign of December 1918, in which I took an active and, as it turned out, rather hazardous part, I packed a lot of learning into two or three weeks.

A General Election in Tiger Bay

When Lloyd George dissolved Parliament on the 25th November, 1918 I had been employed at Cardiff Docks for exactly three weeks. Coming straight into this world of commerce from village life and farmwork, with its mangold pulling, hedge trimming and dung-carting, I was physically and mentally clumsy and, not knowing the rules of the game, my days were a succession of blunders and mishaps. Naturally, I became very disheartened. I had no idea of the rules of precedence and deferred to everyone with a top hat or a bowler. Anyone so hatted could command my immediate attention and subservience. So far as I was concerned they were all officers. A boy from a public school would have detected degrees of consequence and responded accordingly. But had I been more sophisticated I would have dodged one of the most fascinating experiences of my life—electioneering in Tiger Bay at a time when it was known world-wide for its sleazy ill-fame. To-day Tiger Bay is domesticated and respectable in comparison.

It came about like this. Lloyd George's dissolution of Parliament, just fourteen days after the Armistice, caught the political parties unprepared and there was a scramble to form committees and recruit party workers. In South Cardiff the Conservatives had managed to retain a skeleton organization and party workers were not difficult to find in the prosperous suburb of Penarth, which was part of the constituency, but there were relatively few volunteers in Grangetown and Adamsdown and only two for Tiger Bay and the Docks area, of whom I was one.

The Member was standing again and in desperation the divisional party leaders called on his office staff for volunteers. A number offered their services and chose their hunting grounds. Aged sixteen and a half, innocent and ignorant but anxious to please and for experience, I put up my hand and was posted to the Tiger Bay Committee Room for evening and Saturday duty. Looking back, I can only regard the appointment of a boy of that age to share control of a Committe Room at night in the heart of one of the most notorious social black spots in the whole world as a comment on conditions at that time. It was called a Committee Room but as far as I can recall no Committee ever met there; at least not at night. The only other custodian was a Mr. Hirst. He was a Yorkshireman and a former professional cricketer for that county.

As steward of a Conservative Club at the Docks his presence was required there every night from about 6.30 onwards. I usually arrived at the Committee Room about six o'clock, having had some sort of tea in a cafe. There would be talk about canvassers (of whom there were few) and other matters for about half an hour and then he would leave me to hold the fort alone until about 9 p.m. when I would shut up shop and head for my lodgings at Barry. Thus it was that he took the day shift and I the night one.

I think it is true to claim that in 1918 Tiger Bay reached the height of its ill-fame. By day the area was comparatively peaceful and the burly Cardiff City policemen were able to keep the peace by appearing on the streets in pairs but at night, or so it seemed to me, all hell broke loose and the police patrols, I noticed without much reassurance, often numbered four. When, alone in that so-called Committee Room at night, I sometimes heard a woman screaming, I could not believe that anything less than murder had been committed.

To see Tiger Bay as I saw it in 1918 I cannot do better than quote Howard Spring who, to save tram fares which he could not afford, had walked through the Bay on his way to work almost 20 years earlier.

There was fascination in the walk through Tiger Bay. Chinks and Dagos, Lascars and Levantines, slippered about the faintly evil by-ways that ran off Bute Street. The whole place was a warren of seamen's boarding houses, dubious hotels, ships' chandlers smelling of rope and tarpaulins, shops full of hard flat ships' biscuits, dingy chemists' shops stored with doubtful looking pills, herbs and the works of Aristotle. Children of the strangest colours, fruits of frightful misalliances, staggered half-naked about the streets; and the shop windows were decorated with names that were an epitome of all the clans and classes under the sun. The flags of all nations fluttered from the house fronts; and ever and anon the long bellowing moan of a ship coming to the docks or outward bound seemed the very voice of this meeting place of the seven seas. It was a dirty, smelly, rotten and romantic district, an offence and an inspiration, and I loved it. (From 'Heaven Lies About Us'. Constable & Co. Ltd.)

In the seventeen years since Spring walked through it, the character of the area had not changed; rather it had deepened since four years of war had left it even more sordid and violent.

The Committee Room, situated about half way along Bute Street, was right in the heart of the Bay. A double-fronted lock-up shop, it had last been used by a barber whose pole remained outside. Behind and above was a boarding-house for Spanish seamen, silent by day but noisy at night when some sort of mechanical contraption produced a non-stop rattle of guitar music, accompanied by occasional bursts of male revelry. It was flanked by cafés, shops and boarding houses of the kind described by Spring. Opposite was the long unbroken wall of the railway embankment and behind the railway the West Dock. Because of wartime restrictions the street lighting was dim and, by contrast, the former barber's shop was an island of light in a sea of gloom in those mid-December nights. It was lit by a large hanging gas lamp, controlled by chains. For the first few nights I felt uncomfortably conspicuous as, sitting alone at the trestle table in the middle of the room waiting for canvassers or enquirers, I was conscious of being stared at by black, white, brown and yellow faces through the clear glass of the large window. Hours would pass without a single visitor and I could stand the scrutiny no longer, so providing myself with a pot of paste I covered the windows to a height of six feet with election posters, leaving no peepholes. In spite of this, or because of it, I had trouble on more than one occasion with foreign seamen, drunk or half-drunk who, either on observing the barber's pole or because of past custom, came in for a shave or hair-cut and were reluctant to leave without one.

No canvassers would work in that area at night but one Saturday morning, with Mr. Hirst in charge of the Room, I tried my novice hand, making two calls. On the ground floor shipping department of the company's offices I had often seen a bowler-hatted, dark-overcoated, middle-aged man who, I thought, was a member of the staff as he spent many hours of the day standing in the central passage apparently with nothing to do except occasionally exchange a word or two with the clerks at work at their high desks behind the counters. This was Mr. Pitt, whose job it was to recruit seamen and firemen for the company's fleet and for those other lines for which the company acted as agent. I now think he earned his living from fees collected from the men he took on and that he was no more than a free-lance employment agent, who spent as much time in the local pubs as he did in the office. It was through him that the company got their Chinese and Lascar crews and he was therefore well known to, and on good terms with, the boarding-house keepers who catered for those races. Taking me aside one day, he told me (his breath smelling of alcohol) that I could bring in all the Chinese and Arabs in Tiger Bay on to the Boss's side if I would call on a Chinese boarding-house keeper in what, if I remember rightly, was Patrick Street, and on an Arab hotelier in a street just north of the canal bridge and I was to be sure to say, 'Mr. Pitt sent me.'

At sixteen and fresh from the farm I was in no position to question the value of this suggestion or the authority or judgement of the man who made it. The fact that he was bowler-hatted, wore a dark overcoat and looked important was enough for me. So along I went to Patrick Street, where at the door of a tall, terraced house (formerly the home of a well-to-do middle class family no doubt) I asked by name for the boarding-house keeper. The door had been opened to me by a young Chinaman who was dressed cleanly and neatly in a white shirt with a black tie and black trousers. Smiling, he invited me into a front room as I explained that I had been sent along by Mr. Pitt of .... Shipowners, whereupon he smiled more warmly. What I had expected to see in the front room of a Chinese seamen's boarding-house I don't know. What I now saw astonished me. The high-ceilinged, well-proportioned room seemed, to my rustic eyes, the embodiment of opulence with its heavy curtains, deep carpeting and comfortable sofas and easy chairs. I was told to sit on a sofa while a search was made for the owner. On entering the dimly-lit room I thought I was its only occupant, but as soon as I sat down I saw I was not alone. Crouched before a blazing fire at the far end was a young white woman who showed no awareness of my presence but continued to sit there, still and silent, staring into the fire. She was wearing a dressing gown or bath robe and presented a picture of such deep dejection and hopeless misery that I felt very sorry for her. From the hall came sounds of excited Chinese voices and a Chinese head or two peered in at me for a second or so and vanished. With a sense of dismay I realised that my mention of the name of my shipowning employers had suggested to them that jobs were on offer. The minutes ticked on and with a mounting sense of panic I was finding it harder and harder to resist an impulse to make a dash for the front door when that door was opened and slammed shut by a young lady who stamped into the room in a blaze of anger. I call her a lady since she was wearing a fur coat. (In my eyes in those days only ladies wore fur coats; certainly no women in my range of acquaintance possessed one). But this was no lady. Ignoring me as if I were invisible, as the other had done, she gave vent to a torrent of invective in an attempt to invoke the sympathy of her dejected friend before the fire. Her words shocked me, for though common enough among the colliers and farm-workers among whom I had lived I had never heard them from the lips of a woman, and this woman was young and rather pretty. The burden of her complaint was that she had wished to go into the town to do some shopping but that 'bugger' (here she mentioned what sounded like a Chinese name) had followed her closely up Bute Street and she had been forced to return to get rid of the 'bugger'. This was too much for me and I had almost reached the front door when the young man who had ushered me in met me, still smiling, and told me the proprietor could not be found and that he must have been out. Promising to return, I got out and failed to keep my promise.

For any sensible boy that attempt at canvassing should have been enough to discourage all approaches to foreign boarding-houses in Tiger Bay but, ever dutiful, I went along to the Arab one, which claimed the higher status of an hotel. Here, I got no further than the hallway, which was far enough for me for I was met not only with a cordial greeting and promise of support from the smiling proprietor but also with a really offensive smell, which seemed to pervade my being for days afterwards, yet the place looked clean as did the proprietor. Describing it to friends, some said it came from the oils used by Arabs for cooking; others thought it was from the oil that Arabs rubbed over their bodies. Perhaps both schools of thought were correct and that the same oils served both purposes. That Arab was as good as his word—at least he turned up at the booth on polling day!

I now wonder how many Cardiff Chinese and Arabs had votes in 1918. I must have checked the Register of Electors before making these approaches, and there were 'Chinks, Lascars and Levantines' in Tiger Bay, as Howard Spring says, in 1901, which would have allowed them plenty of time to multiply and qualify.

I remember only one active canvasser, an Army Officer on leave, who told me that he had found the ladies of the Bay very welcoming. He should have restricted his interest in them to those aged 30 and over, for in this, the first election in which women had the vote, those under 30 were deemed to be so devoid of a responsible attitude to politics as not to merit the privilege. The 'Flapper Vote' came later.

One evening, as I took over from Mr. Hirst he mentioned that a torchlight procession in support of the Liberal candidate was to pass along Bute Street later that night. The said candidate was a man called Curran, owner of a local engineering factory, which had been heavily engaged in the manufacture of munitions during the war and still employed a large number of women workers who, in loyalty to their employer, were organizing the procession. I had taken Mr. Hirst's mention of the procession as a casual remark, merely for my information, but as the time of the procession drew near I began to feel that it had been intended as a warning. For a couple of hours my vigil was uneventful. There were the usual noises: the unceasing guitar music from the Spaniards behind the shop, the grind and clanging of tram-cars as they hurried by, shunting engines on the docks opposite, the sirens of arriving and departing ships and the shriller shrieks of their attendant tugs and, continuously at that time of night, the voices of passers-by, none in Welsh, some in English, but mostly foreign and male. There were, as usual, no callers and I sat there alone.

Towards nine o'clock I heard the sound of some band instruments and some rather ragged singing and, going outside, saw the head of the procession coming from the direction of Pier Head. In the light of the carried torches I could see the fawn overalls of women munition workers. I went back inside, locked the door and, vaguely apprehensive, waited for the procession to pass. It didn't. On reaching the brightly lit room, with its 'Vote Conservative' posters, the procession halted to boo and shout and scream. Mingling with the shrill voices of the women were men's voices, gruff and hoarse and foreign, and they did not sound too friendly. In its progress through Tiger Bay, the cavalcade, composed mostly of young women, had attracted a following of foreign seamen who, as was now plain, were willing to give all the support of which they were capable, whatever the cause, and here was their chance to do so. Encouraged by the boos and shouts of the women the newly recruited Liberals banged with their fists on the windows and hammered and pushed at the door. All held until someone booted in a large hole in the glass flanking one side of the entrance through which I snatched a glimpse of the legs of men straining at the door. I had had enough. I had not imagined any such happening and so had made no plan of action. What followed was purely instinctive. A sharp tug on the 'off' chain controlling the gas lamp put the place in darkness—there was little or no light coming in from the street. In the same movement I unlocked the door and raised the latch whereupon the pushers tumbled and stumbled in and in the darkness and confusion I was lost among them. I was the first out and once clear of the crowd took to my heels up Bute Street towards the relative safety of Custom House Street, not pausing to seek sanctuary or to report the matter to Bute Street Police Station, which was not far from the scene of mayhem. In doing so I overtook a number of fawn-clad women and a bandsman or two who 'stood not upon the order of their going' but went—the support given to them by these new-found sympathisers had been more than they had bargained for. The noise they made had certainly been frightening, although the damage was relatively small. True a large window pane had been smashed, but inside there was little to knock about. Chairs and trestle-tables had been overturned, inkpots upset and ink splashes everywhere, and piles of leaflets scattered and trodden upon. I took time off the following morning to clear up the mess.

The incident was reported in the Cardiff newspapers. In one of them a reporter had asked the wife of the Conservative candidate if she had any comment to make. She said she welcomed the incident: it showed that people were at last taking an interest in the Election. I could have told her that it was unlikely that those who had busted up the Committee Room had a single vote among them. They were foreign seamen stranded in Tiger Bay and longing for a bit of excitement, especially any that would find favour with the ladies.

The Member won the Election and on Polling Day gave me a red, white and blue rosette in recognition of my services to the Cause! Soon afterwards he was further gratified on being created a baronet, but for what services or what benefaction I can't now remember. Until then he had been for some years a mere knight and in those post-war days knights at Cardiff Docks were two-a-penny and not without good reason was Cardiff known as 'the City of Dreadful Knights.'

He also retained his seat in the next General Election, that of November 1922. I have in front of me as I write his Election Address on

70

that occasion, which bears all the marks of having been written by a party hack: it was certainly beyond his powers of composition. In it he advocates lower taxation, the avoidance of 'expensive experiments' (of what sort is not specified) and the exercise of 'most strict economy.' And then with a sublime lack of sincerity he went on to say, 'The interests of the constituency and my interests are inseparable. I share your reverses; I share your successes.' But not, as one could so easily have pointed out, in equal measure. There was much unemployment and poverty in Cardiff in 1922 (the decline in the coal industry had begun), particularly in the working class parts of the constituency. And in that Election he learned, greatly to his cost, that his interests and those of his constituents were not inseparable. One night, coming out of a public meeting in Grangetown, a part of the city where in the long terraced streets there was much evidence of hardship, he was jostled by an unfriendly crowd, which was unnerving but not unusual, and he attributed the incident to his political opponents until he got home and discovered that his magnificent pearl tie-pin was missing. He then realised that the jostling had been a cover for the snatch. Next day, a newspaper placard on the stand outside his office said 'Candidate loses £600 Tie-pin.' Now, sixty years later, I suppose its present value could be put at about £10,000. The photograph on his Election Address shows the huge pearl: it had been a present from his second wife and it was a grievous loss to them. A man so lacking in imagination as to wear jewellery of this sort at a political meeting in a part of the city where people were ill-fed, shabbily clothed and badly housed, surely deserved to lose not only the gem but also his seat in the House of Commons, and he did so in the General Election that followed a year later.

It was this sort of experience with my first employers that established my sense of values—I had almost none when I joined the firm. I began to see that men holding public positions of some eminence, even if put there by the democratic process of balloting, might yet be self-seeking, vain and stupid.

It quickly became obvious to me that the secretary, Mr. Annear, was in every way superior to those he acknowledged as his 'superiors,' in intelligence, wisdom and judgement, even as a public speaker, although he took no part in politics. Yet he deferred to the inferior man as an employee (he would not have been ashamed to use the word servant) and as a Christian. Apart from other considerations, such as the need to earn a living, he held it was an employee's duty at all times to serve one's boss

71

(whether a man or corporation) loyally and to the best of one's ability, so long as one's duties did not conflict with the Christian conscience.

A lot of my subsequent 'yesmanship' stemmed from this training. To some it must have looked like sycophancy but I knew what I was doing and why. I was paid to be hardworking, honest and loyal, and I tried to give value for money and perhaps, sometimes, I gave more than I received in rewards.

THE PLYMOUTH BROTHER

Seven days after I began work, the war of 1914-18 came to an end with the signing of the Armistice. News of its impending signature was conveyed to me by the Commissionaire whose duties included those of telephone operator of the private branch exchange in his cubby hole downstairs. I was to inform the secretary, which I did. He received the news impassively—it had been expected—and he resumed his dictation. It was not long before the Commissionaire rang again with the news that a short service was to be held on the floor of the Exchange at eleven o'clock. I communicated this message also to the secretary and again it was received with little show of interest. But I was expected and requested permission for myself and my seventeen-year-old colleague to attend. He asseted and shortly before eleven o'cloch we hurried over to the Exchange and took up our positions on the top gallery amid growing excitement as the floor filled with dark suited men, all bowler-hatted or top-hatted, and the galleries filled with the underlings—clerks, book-keepers, typists and messengers. Just before eleven o'clock a small procession, headed by our company chairman who was also chairman of the Exchange, took up positions on the dais. And as the hands of the large clock pointed to the hour he announced the coming into effect of the Armistice. The news was received in silence: too many present had losts sons, brothers, friends for cheering.

I vaguely recall the Vicar of St. Stephen's offering a prayer before the Chairman announced that they would mark the occasion by singing 'O God our help in ages past.' There was no accompaniment and no hymnbooks. It didn't matter: the tune and words were familiar to all, the hymn having been sung so often during those terrible four years. As someone pitched the tune, the Chairman removed his hat, whereupon we, looking down from above, saw a black sea transformed by a wave-like motion into a greyish-white sea as all on the floor did likewise, revealing bald pates or grey or white hair. Few young members were able to be present in November 1918. The hymn was sung magnificently. Begun on the floor by male voices only, it was taken up by the men and women and boys and girls in the galleries. It was followed by another general movement on the floor as the members put on their hats and many took out their handkerchiefs, for the hymn and the manner of its singing had stirred deep emotions. For a few magical moments that Temple of Mammon had been transformed into what for many of us was an evocation of a chapel in the valleys on the occasion of a singing festival, a Gymanfa Ganu.

As eyes were dried and noses blown we wondered, what next? To return to our desks and typewriters was unthinkable. The Chairman ended the uncertainty by announcing that he would lead a procession to the City Hall where they would pay their respects to the Lord Mayor and invited all present to go with him. This invitation I now believe was intended for the members of the Exchange only, but we outsiders in the galleries thought it applied to us also. Thus was formed one of the strangest processions that city has ever seen. At the head of it, top-hatted or bowler-hatted, the leading members of the Docks establishment, the shipowners and colliery owners, all rich men, followed closely by their principal henchmen, lawyers, stockbrokers, merchants of various kinds and the lesser members of the Exchange, and behind them, the clerks, book-keepers and typists, with junior clerks and office boys forming a lively tail. Thus it began, but during its peregrination through Tiger Bay it attracted the interest and support of numbers of foreign seamen, of all races and colours, so that instead of being at the end of the procession I saw on looking behind that I was now in the middle of it. Certainly the invitation had not been extended to this .notley lot! On arriving at the City Hall it was obvious that it had not included us underlings either. Where the point of cut-off came or who decided it, I don't know, but my colleague and I were certainly numbered among the hoi polloi and left to find our own pleasures on that dull and miserable November day. Apart from the overflowing pubs barred to us both by law and inclination, Cardiff offered no distractions and I returned early to my dismal lodgings, hungry and dispirited.

Next morning as my colleague and I turned up for work we were sharply reprimanded by the secretary, Mr. Annear, for failing to return to the office after the ceremony on 'Change to which his consent had been restricted: he had waited for us until early afternoon before packing up and going home. We said we had accepted the invitation of

73

the Chairman to join the march to the City Hall. This innocent answer defeated him. I think we were more surprised by his remaining at work than he was by our desertion.

Few had continued at work in the offices after eleven o'clock on Armistice Day and the fact that he had done so can be attributed to his being a leading member of the sect known among themselves as 'The Brethren' and to others as Plymouth Brethren. For him, and them, being 'saved' involved separation, so far as they could manage it under ordinary conditions of life, from the 'world.' This meant renunciation of such pleasures as theatre-going and the reading of novels. It also meant non-participation in politics and national celebrations such as the Armistice. He belonged to another Kingdom: that of Christ. I noted that summer holidays by the sea and playing golf were not included in the Index. He did not explain these attitudes to me: I got to know them from observing what he did and did not do and what he said to others.

Aged about 60, he was strikingly handsome and most distinguished in his bearing, being tall, well built, even rather portly, and erect. Always immaculately dressed, his well-cut clothes were provided by a tailor who waited upon him in the office, with cloth samples and tape measure. His boots (business men did not wear shoes in those days), set off with pale grey or fawn spats, were also bespoke and came from a London firm of bootmakers, Dowie and Marshall, who, I was to discover later, also made the boots of two subsequent employers, both men of title and substance.

Mr. Annear had another patrician habit. Work at the office began, nominally at least, at nine o'clock, but he got there, travelling first-class in a 'workers'' train shortly after 8.30. Receiving the letters for the senior directors and himself from the Commissionaire he opened as many as appeared to him to be of interest or importance. At nine o'clock he was there to check that his underlings were punctual and if I were late, as too often I was, his displeasure and reprimand terrified me. At five minutes past nine he would don his Homburg hat, with its silk-edged brim, made, I saw, by Stetson (another example of his insistence on having the best) and walk over to Edward Roberts' establishment in Mount Stuart Square, where behind a smart outfitter's department, in a luxuriously appointed saloon, three or four smiling barbers were ready to welcome him. He knew them all by their Christian names, was really interested in them and their families, and in return they esteemed him highly, and accorded him the greatest respect, considering it an honour to wait on him. How do I know? Occasionally, a cable or telegram or some other urgent message would require his immediate attention when it fell to me to take his instructions while still receiving the attention of the barbers. (I observed the same attitude of liking and respect on the part of station-masters down to porters and cab drivers. In those early post-war days horse-drawn cabs, hansoms and 'growlers', stood in West Bute Street and when sent to fetch one for him, and in reply to the cabbie's 'Who for?' I said 'Mr. Annear', there was always a reaction of pleasure which, I was sure, was not wholly attributable to expectation of a generous tip. His distinguished appearance graced the dingiest of cabs: his good humour and friendliness—perhaps loving kindness would be nearer the mark—meant that any act of service to him was attended by pleasure).

Returning to the office about 9.30 with hair, beard and moustache perfectly trimmed and pomaded, and his pink cheeks 'smooth as a baby's bottom', he would settle down for the day's work. But another piece of ritual had to be performed first. On the side of his large roll-top desk he had a pipe stand with several fine pipes from which he made a careful choice. Then from a desk drawer came a bright blue tin of Edgeworth Slice tobacco (the best ever, according to my father, an authority on the subject) and only when the pipe had been carefully filled and was drawing nicely would dictation begin. Then in a haze of blue, sweet-smelling tobacco smoke he said what he had to say steadily, kindly tempering his speed to my own in shorthand writing at the time. I never sat to receive dictation as secretaries do nowadays if television stories tell the truth, but stood, resting my book on the top of his roll-top desk. Twenty years later in another job I was required to do likewise for a time.

The correspondence was extremely varied. It ranged over matters arising from the normal duties of a company secretary (and he was secretary to many companies) such as the transfer and transmission of shares, preparation for, and attendance at, Board and other meetings, and the control and custody of investments, but also covered the business correspondence of the two principal directors which, in my time, included the parliamentary correspondence of the Member, mostly letters from and to aggrieved constituents, and with government ministers on their behalf. It was a good training.

In retrospect, two facts seem to be worth mentioning. First, the relative lightness of the parliamentary mail in the five years immediately following the first world war compared with the deluge of letters from aggrieved constituents received by another Conservative

M.P. after the second world war, whom I served in precisely the same capacity as had Mr. Annear, twenty years earlier. And now, sixty years on, if Members' statements in support of claims for larger and larger grants towards secretarial help are founded on fact, more and more people are finding cause for belly-aching groans, mostly due, I suppose, to some mismanagement, true or alleged, in some department of government. In 1920 there were fewer bureaucrats to make mistakes and, I believe, a greater readiness to stand on one's own feet. If we are poor, ill-fed or unemployed, that is lacking in bread and circuses, it's always the fault of the Government! In the nineteen-twenties, when Norman Tebbit's father was unemployed he got on his bike and looked for work: when later in the nineteen-twenties I became unemployed, it never occurred to me to blame the Government, so I went back to farmwork (unpaid) to toughen myself up for farmwork in Canada—but that's another story. By to-day's standards Norman's dad and I were prize fools.

The other fact is that Members of Parliament with other interests, business or otherwise, have little time to spare for dealing with complaints, personal or general, brought before them by constituents. It was so forty years ago, and the position must have worsened since. Hence the need for secretaries, but in 1920 I was surprised to find that letters to constituents and to the Minister whose department was alleged to have been at fault were written and signed in the Member's name by the private secretary. Not that this made any difference to the outcome: the secretary I was serving was better at letter writing than his master, the response from the Minister would be no less factual, thoroughly researched and politely expressed (I never failed to admire the quality of the ministerial secretaries) and in my experience the Member always saw what had been done in his name and on his behalf. But in the case of our Member, I never remember his writing a single letter—at the time I did not think it was at all odd, believing that there was no point in barking oneself if one kept a dog, but I have since wondered, Member of Parliament though he was, whether he had the mental equipment and education to do so!

I typed on an antiquated, very heavy, Smith Premier machine with a double keyboard (capitals as well as lower case letters), to-day a museum piece. Also a museum piece, as I recently saw one in an antique dealer's shop, was our letter copying press. The carbon copying system had not been adopted in that office at that time (Dickensian methods still prevailed) and my colleague who was even more inclined to be slap-dash than I was, and I quailed every time the boss asked to see the letter book. Typed letters presented little difficulty as the ink on the typewriter ribbon was designed to reproduce itself clearly in the process of copying, but the hand-written ones needed very careful handling. The letter was placed face downwards on a numbered page of fine tissue paper (we couldn't tear out a spoiled copy without the risk of discovery and condign punishment). Behind the page was placed a dampened square of blue cotton cloth and behind that again an impervious oiled card, and providing we had enough cloths and cards, we could copy more than a dozen letters at a time. If the cloths were too dry, the copies would be so faint as to be indecipherable; if too wet, the results would be smudgy, possibly illegible, and the letters themselves smudged and limp. Whatever the pressure for speed (a Saturday afternoon football or cricket match or an evening engagement) it was a job that could not be hurried. The press had to be turned down gently, otherwise the book and all within it would tend to twist and both letters and copies would suffer. And all too often we were in a hurry. So, when the boss called for the letter book, we (my seventeen-year-old colleague and I) waited in dread for the shout summoning us to read aloud a letter that had suffered in our hands in the process of copying. When we could not read or invent what was on the page we were given a verbal lashing that made me squirm for hours afterwards. I knew he had right on his side, but what I felt was unfair was his apparent indifference to the question of guilt: he never asked which one of us had made a hash of the copying. More often than not my colleague and friend was the guilty party, so I then made it my sole responsibility, while he did the filing of incoming letters.

Soon I was instructed in the art of writing minutes based on notes made by the chief in the Agenda books used at Annual General Meetings and Board Meetings. Most of the decisions and resolutions were stereotyped and presented no difficulty and the chief dictated any unusual or difficult minute. On one memorable occasion I made a mistake and erased it and wrote carefully over it, hoping it would not be noticed. It was, and the row that followed ensured that I would never forget that among the worst crimes to which a company secretary might be tempted was to erase and try to cover up part of an entry in a minute book.

I was instructed in the routine of dealing with the transfer and transmission of shares, from the examination of transfers and probates to the filling-in in my best handwriting of share certificates before signature and sealing by directors and secretary, the secretary always insisting that I relock the seals in his presence after use, for they, he explained, were what gave the certificates their validity—not the signatures. Sixty years on it might well be wondered why a boy of seventeen, and an inefficient one at that, should be engaged in duties of such importance. The answer is that this was 1919 and there was no-one else available as the former under-secretaries were slow to be 'demobbed' and some had been killed. I remember looking with admiration in the minute books at the particularly fine handwriting of someone who had been there only a year or so earlier and being told that it was the work of a young man, not much older than myself, who had been killed in action just before I was taken on.

Where it may be asked were the women and girls? So far as that firm was concerned they were in their proper places—in the home or serving in shops or, in the case of the directors, on the stage. This was a place for men only and I could not imagine it otherwise. Everything in the office in 1918 had been as it was when that building was first occupied in 1899 apart from the lighting, electricity having supplanted gas. The book-keepers on the second floor still worked standing up at their high desks as did the shipping clerks on the ground floor. Telephones were little used: for local communication personal contact on the floor of the Exchange or inter-office visits were preferred and for long distance and overseas we relied on telegrams and cables. The secretary would not have a telephone in his room and, when necessary, which by present standards was seldom, used the instrument on the high desk at which I worked.

Mr. Annear's working day ended when he had signed all the letters, that is any time between 3.30 and 5.30. My colleague and I for the time being, left after we had copied them (we were forbidden to copy them before signing: in any case the damp process made it impracticable) 'put them up' with their proper enclosures, stamped and entered them in the stamp book, which often meant our having to work until after 6.30 on week-days and sometimes until after one o'clock on Saturdays. There was no overtime pay but we could claim, if kept very late, tea money, normally sixpence. Coffee breaks in the morning and tea breaks in the afternoon were unheard of: anyhow there was no woman in the place for this or any other chore of this nature.

For a time—I can't recall whether it covered months or years—Mr. Annear took a Turkish Bath in a health clinic in St. John's Square, owned and managed by a Mr. Petersen, father of Jack, who later became a champion heavy-weight boxer. These sessions were timed for late afternoon and if any important letters requiring his signature had not been ready when he left in a horse drawn cab or a taxi it fell to my lot to follow him in a Pier Head tram an hour or so later. There in a cooling-off cubicle, my respected boss, swathed in towels, would read the letters carefully while I waited in dread for the explosion that erupted on the discovery of any error. Happiness for me was the silence that betokened approval and the request for the fountain pen. Then back on the tram to the office to finish the day's work. A patrician habit that one would not normally associate with a leading member of the Plymouth Brethren sect! Nor one for which young lady secretaries would be better suited to take my place! In that establishment also I was conscious of the respect and affection this man inspired in all who waited upon him, from Mr. Petersen downwards.

The ground floor of the office was laid out rather like an old-style bank, with a central passage between two well polished counters and, behind the counters, the long high desks at which the chartering clerks and others stood to work. At the end of the passage a door led into the shipping manager's office which was screened off from the rest of the ground floor by a tall partition of opaque glass. At the other end, near the entrance lobby was a wide open staircase leading to the floors above and from it one had a fine view of all that was going on, or not going on, over the whole of the ground floor apart from the manager's office. That staircase was the stage for a piece of theatre in which I had only a walking-on part but for me it was an awesome occasion, never forgotten by me and long remembered by others who witnessed it. The drama or comedy—call it what you will—arose out of ignorance. I had been in this strange world for some months, but I was still 'green' and easily bluffed. The secretary had asked me to go down to the shipping department (there was no 'inter-com.' system in those offices at that time) and find out from the clerks there the position of one of the company's vessels. This request was unusual as normally the whereabouts of the ships did not concern him, but he never asked for anything without good reason. The first clerk I approached said he didn't know, so I went to another working a few feet away and he didn't know either. A third, who had heard the response of the others, gave the same answer. Returning to the boss I told him, 'They don't know where the S.S. R........ is, Sir.' 'Who doesn't know?' he asked. I named the three young men, whereupon he just said, 'Come with me!' We got half way down the open staircase when he stopped with me beside him. Then in stentorian voice he called the name of the shipping manager, 'Mr. Hopkins!' It was mid-morning and the office was full, not only with the usual staff but also with ships' officers, and clerks and messengers from other offices. The talk, movement and sound of typewriters stopped abruptly and was replaced with a hush of expectancy like that in a theatre on the rise of the curtain for the first act. Into this silence and stillness, Mr. Hopkins, a man in late middle age, came slowly into sight at the door of his office, surprise and puzzlement expressed in every line of his countenance. On seeing Mr. Annear on the staircase he essayed a few steps towards him only to be stopped in his tracks. 'Stay where you are, Mr. Hopkins!' the boss thundered, and added, 'I sent Arthur to enquire the position of the S.S. R........ He asked Squire, Foxhall and Murdoch and they all said they didn't know. Will you please let me have the information within the next few minutes?' The manager meekly apologised on behalf of his staff, the three clerks named kept their heads well down, and the answer came almost as soon as the boss and I got back to his room.

In my long working life with aristocratic, autocratic and even mildly eccentric employers, I have been reprimanded justly and sometimes unjustly (or so I felt) on a number of occasions and I have seen many other underlings—porters, waiters, chauffeurs, butlers, maids—receiving verbal lashings delivered by men and, occasionally women, masterly in the art of reprimanding, but I have never seen reproof more stylishly and effectively delivered. Would such a scene be possible to-day in any office or factory? I doubt it: complaints must go through 'the usual channels' and in writing!

I recall another occasion when he delivered a reproof in circumstances that called for some degree of moral courage. He was listening, apparently patiently, to a former sea captain who, retiring early, had established himself in some sort of business at the Docks, a choleric character, given to vehement speech, and a person not amenable to correction of any sort, and I, working silently, at my desk in the next room, was listening avidly to a grievance he had come to air, in the course of which he exclaimed 'Good God!' 'Stop!' said Mr. Annear, 'You mustn't take God's name in vain!' That verbal upper-cut as sharp as it was unexpected, set the astonished captain back on his heels and there was a perceptive pause before he said 'Sorry' and continued with his complaint in a milder tone.

In the sixty years since those days I have known many men who, by their achievements in politics, the armed services or in business, have won my admiration and respect, but none stands higher in my estimation than William Powell Annear, for in that particularly difficult environment he allowed neither praise nor profit to warp his judgements, influence his indomitable integrity or deaden his sense of compassion for those hurt in life's struggle. He had known, so he told me, extreme poverty as a young married man with a young and large family to support. On one occasion, while unemployed, he had gone home penniless knowing that there was no food in the house and that his children were hungry. That experience had bitten deep but had not embittered him as it would a lesser man. It had made him more mindful of the sufferings of others as I knew from errands of mercy with food or money for people in need on which I was sometimes sent. Nor had comparative comfort, indeed some small luxuries like his shaving habit, his fine clothes, his Turkish baths and his Saturday golf, spoiled him in any way. He never owned a car, preferring to travel in trams, buses or trains, or, if necessary, taxis. In accordance with the tradition of the Brethren he gave not less than ten per cent of his income ('the tithe' as he called it) 'to the Lord's work.' Whether this was based on gross income or the income left after tax I never enquired, but in those days income tax was not the big factor it has since become. His was a prestigious figure by nature and by nobility of character and, while others around him sought riches and fame, he was content to take what he was given and not always as much as that, as he turned down an offer of a decoration from the King for services to commerce during the war.

As I approached and passed the age he was when I knew him, I remembered with increasing admiration the example he set of complete integrity, especially when, in business, I was faced with roughly similar situations and problems. I recall his consideration for the well-being of others, particularly those subject to his authority, as I was, his real interest in all sorts and conditions of men, showing no more respect to the rich than to the poor, and his capacity for doing good by stealth.

Of him his children's children can be justly proud but he set standards dauntingly hard for us who succeed him to attain.

Ten years after I left the firm he died aged 80 and I travelled to Cardiff for his funeral. On boarding a bus at Kingsway to take me to Llandaff where the service was to be held, the bus conductor, noting my black tie and my destination, asked me, 'Are you going to the old gentleman's funeral?' 'Yes,'—there was no need to ask what old gentleman. Wondering how the conductor came to know him, he told me that he had travelled on the buses 'and we all thought him the nicest chap alive.'

I could imagine his doing so, smiling, courteous and kind and most distinguished looking withal.

Winners and Losers

Whatever one's place in the hierarchy of that business world, one rule seemed to over-ride all others—that of 'keeping up an appearance.' I saw that all the older members of the staff, whatever their status, put on a show of importance and behaved as if they were already managers or managerial material. They dressed expensively and displayed a degree of dignity, quite out of keeping with their routine duties and inferior status. Occasionally, some in their fifties or early sixties, despairing of promotion, accepted defeat and lapsed into the category of the shabby-genteel, and pathetic figures they were. Their misery was plain and I felt sorry for them. It is one thing to be poor among the very poor: it is quite a different thing to be poor when rubbing shoulders daily with the very rich. Sometimes the pretence was taken to absurd lengths. I knew a man, who, holding a modest position and being paid accordingly, felt that he could not afford a mid-day meal at a restaurant of a quality conforming to his idea of his importance, and disdaining to take sandwiches as most junior clerks and office boys had to do, scurried to catch a mid-day train to his home ten miles away, there to snatch a hasty lunch, and scurried back again. There were no staff canteens, and mid-day trains from Clarence Road and Bute Street Stations catered for this habit.

Contrary to the belief of most Cardiff people, salaries and wages of 'docksmen' (not dockers!) in the city's dockland, a place with a reputation for sprouting millionaires like mushrooms after rain on a warm September night, were generally shockingly low as I was learning in respect of myself. Beginning with a wage of five shillings a week, raised to seven shillings and six pence three months later and probably to ten shillings after six months, all these increments, according to the agenda and minute books, having first been solemnly considered by the millionaire directors, I got a bit restive after a year or so when my pay was, I suppose, about the £1 mark and I must have spoken to the boss rather more boldly about it than he expected. He listened patiently to what I had to say and answered kindly to the effect that he understood my position, but I should try to appreciate how the directors and he viewed the position. They could not consider need, and the basis of their awards was parity among the junior clerks in the various departments. If one got out of step all the rest would expect to be treated likewise. And then he played his trump card. Did I realise that there were many boys leaving the Grammar Schools of the area, particularly Cardiff High School, whose parents would gladly pay for the sort of training I was receiving? I did, and shut up.

One junior tried to supplement his poor pay by faking the stamp book. The coal exporting department sent out weekly circulars to foreign customers quoting prices for the various grades of Welsh coal. The postage on them was fairly considerable, at least in the eyes of the junior clerk, so for a number of weeks he pitched the circulars into the coke burning furnace in the basement and pocketed the stamp money. All went well until customers abroad began to complain about the failure of the price list to reach them. This was at a time when it was almost as difficult to sell Welsh coal overseas as it was to sell fur coats to South Sea Islanders and the junior despatch clerk, whose visits to the cellar had aroused the curiosity of the commissionaire, was himself despatched.

In 1919 or 1920 there was a clerks' strike at Cardiff Docks. For clerks to strike was an unheard of thing in those days and it caused sensation. Cory Brothers, a large colliery owning and shipping firm, under the personal control of members of the Cory family (they, too, were of Cornish stock) had honoured their promise to take back into their employment all men who had served in the Armed Forces during the war and whose service pay they had supplemented to bring it to the level at which it stood when they joined up. These men were now several years older and there had been some inflation in prices but the rises in salary they had been given (if any) bore little relation to what the men felt they deserved. The Corys (of Cory Brothers) had a great reputation in the area for benevolence (among their benefactions was the Cory Hall, built and maintained for the promotion of temperance) and I have no doubt that Sir Reginald Cory and his co-directors felt that they had dealt fairly with all members of their staff, but my experience has been that when men have become very rich they have difficulty in realising that for a man earning fifty shillings a week a reduction to forty-five shillings could mean penury while an additional five shillings might appear to him as near affluence.

Cory Brothers were used to strikes at their collieries, but one in their own head office could not be true! It was and, sharing a measure of disbelief myself, I went along to Bute Street to see for myself the groups of striking clerks and a disconsolate lot they were, shamefaced and plainly worried by their staggering audacity. Sixty-five years later they would have been more brazen about it—bank clerks, teachers and even doctors have, with much less cause, made striking almost respectable.

What happened to Cory Brothers' clerks as a result of the strike I can't recall; possibly the terms of the settlement (if any) were never published, but one thing is certain: many lost their jobs not long afterwards, not so much as a punishment for their act of bravado, but as a consequence of long and bitter strikes in the company's collieries (as well as throughout the coalfield) combined with a sharply falling demand for coal, especially the bunker coals in which the firm specialised. This was the beginning of the great dispersal from Cardiff Docks. The South Wales coal trade and its dependent shipping and ship repair yards were all badly hit long before the years of the slump. Of the many young hopefuls of my own age that I got to know at Cardiff Docks in the years 1918 to 1923 I can't remember one who was there in 1925. There was a great exodus: some went overseas but most went over the border to England.

In 1919 or 1920, when I was still earning not more than £1 a week and so unable to maintain myself, I received, quite unexpectedly, an addition to my pay equivalent to roughly half a year's earnings, a cheque for £25. 'What's this for?' I asked the accountant who had handed it to me. 'For you,' he said. 'But why?' 'Because of E.P.T.,' he replied. E.P.T. stood for Excess Profits Tax which was to be levied on the firm in respect of the enormous profits that had fallen to its lot during the war. I say 'fallen to its lot' because that phrase expresses the true position more precisely than the word 'earned'.

This amazing windfall filled my head with ideas as to how I might best use it—not spend it. I now thought of myself as a capitalist and, being already infected with the get-rich-quick bug then rampant in the fevered atmosphere around me, looked round with a view to discovering a promising investment (whereas common sense indicated the Post Office Savings Bank). But I was in an environment where there was much talk of fortunes being made overnight, and I was eighteen years of age. The gift, for so I regarded it, coincided with the issue of a prospectus for shares in a company called Tankers, Limited which aroused much interest in the office, but not, I should add, in the mind of the secretary who seemed content just to earn his salary. Among the rest of us the general feeling was that Tankers, Limited was bound to succeed. Coal was finished as a bunker fuel: the future was with oil and the tankers to carry it. I was all for investing £20 in Tankers, Limited but my parents had other ideas and I, being still largely dependent on them had to submit. So the money was wholly spent on clothes for myself and my brothers and my chance of making a fortune was lost. It was not long, however, before Tankers, Limited fell victim to the developing recession and those of my colleagues who had put all or some of their E.P.T. bonus in that 'certainty' felt badly let down. But I had benefited in two ways: I had got much needed clothes and, perhaps even more important, a salutary lesson.

How much the others got from the E.P.T. distribution I never knew but as I was, I think, the youngest employee my £25 would have been the minimum and I assumed those earning four times as much had received a correspondingly larger amount and £100 seemed a lot of money in those days. I understood that if the money so distributed had been retained by the company all of it would have had to be handed over to the Government in tax, so I suppose my thanks were due more to the tax laws than to the directors, who were none the poorer for their show of generosity.

I have mentioned earlier profits that 'had fallen to its lot,' preferring that phrase to the word 'earned.' During the later stages of the 1914-18 War profits from shipping were enormous and seemingly gratuitous as was brought home to me by a chance discovery, a discovery so strange, indeed, that in recent years I have a feeling that it was a dream and not a real happening. Twenty or thirty years ago, however, I was convinced that I had seen what I thought I saw. In the later years of my employment with the company, possibly in 1922 or 1923, when the depression was beginning to bite, I noticed a new 'picture' on the wall of the passage leading to my department. To me it was a problem picture. Someone had gone to the trouble of having a ship's charter framed and exhibited. I wondered why. Ships' charters were the business of the floor below and filling in the blanks was a routine duty of the chartering clerks. What was so special about this one? One day, my curiosity aroused, I stopped and examined it closely, and found that it provided for a ship belonging to the company to sail from a South Wales port to Spain with a cargo of coal at £20 a ton. If the charter was on the basis of cost, insurance and freight (c.i.f.) as almost certainly was the case, how much would the shipowner have got from it? The cost of coal, f.o.b. was I think about £1 a ton at the time. The cost of insurance I couldn't guess, but I knew it was high. The costs of the voyage, a short one, were small:

seamen's pay had remained relatively static in spite of the terrible risks they ran. The tonnage was probably in the region of 4,000 in which case the shipowners would receive £80,000 (a lot of money in those days) from one short voyage of a shabby tramp steamer, less the costs I have mentioned. And there would certainly be a very profitable charter for the return voyage with iron ore or oranges. The clue to the mystery was the date, 1917, the year in which the company lost nine of its ships by mine or torpedo. But why frame it and hang it on the wall?

At the time it was hung, the first wave of the depression had hit the coal and shipping companies badly. Many ships were laid up and losses were beginning to replace profits. Ships' crews had lost their jobs, and clerks and managers were willing to accept reductions in pay rather than lose their jobs, yet very many had to go. In these conditions that £20 a ton charter must have made a very pretty picture indeed. The company existed to make profits and here were profits galore—providing the vessel got to Bilboa or Seville—and even had it failed to do so the voyage was well covered by insurance. It was because many such voyages had been completed that the company had found itself loaded with profits it had not fought for but could not refuse when thrust upon them. And it was such profits that the Government was clawing back by means of the Excess Profits Tax.

I thought I understood why the picture was hanging there; it spoke of the time when all in the garden was lovely, but as the years passed I wondered about the morality of it all. It was undoubtedly horribly insensitive, but the church-going directors and managers could have seen nothing wrong in taking moneys freely offered for the use of their ships or they would not have exhibited this memorial to their highest achievement. In the changed social and economic climate of later years, whenever my thoughts turned to that picture the uglier it became. £20 a ton at Bilboa docks was not only a measure of the Spaniards' desperate need for coal in those days: it was also the measure of the fearful risks undertaken by seamen in taking it there.

I saw that picture sixty years ago. I'm sure it has long since been taken down and destroyed. It was a belated example of an attitude common enough in Victorian times—money honestly obtained indeed but in conditions that for others, produced not gain, but loss and misery.

The Bubble Bursts

I have shown how easy it was in those days to amass a fortune, particularly as a shipowner, but other forms of capitalist enterprise also produced undeserved and unexpected rewards, especially for those who owned collieries, ship-repair yards or engineering factories engaged in producing munitions. There were many who were thus favoured with unaccustomed wealth in South Wales at that time and a number of them gave much of it away to charitable causes, notably to such forms of charity as enabled the donor to attach his name to the gift, such as a hospital ward, a maternity hospital, a children's home and so on. Some also contributed to the funds of the political parties, and Lloyd George found Cardiff a fruitful field in which to dig for his own notorious fund, ostensibly for the Liberal Party, but over which he is reputed to have exercised sole control until years later it ran dry. These acts of benevolence, if of sufficient size, were almost always rewarded by the offer of an honour and Cardiff produced a fantastic crop of Peerages, Baronetcies and Knighthoods during and immediately after the 1914-18 War: the City of Dreadful Knights. In my ignorance I looked on this ennobling process as a tested measure of merit and believed that a Viscount was sure to be esteemed by everyone as superior to a mere Baron and both to Baronets and Knights. When later I served as secretary to a Baron who claimed direct descent from a Norman Knight (if not the Conqueror himself) I was astonished to find that these newly created Lords and Sirs who had risen from the ranks on the strength of war-time acquired wealth were no more respected by him and his friends among the country gentry than if they had remained plain 'misters', and his untitled friends held precedence over them. They might preen themselves and swagger around Cardiff, but they cut no ice in the shires.

With all this money about, Rolls Royces and Daimlers, with liveried chauffeurs, became a common sight in Mount Stuart Square. My first car ride had been in a Model T Ford in 1918: my second was in 1921, when, during a railway strike, I was given a lift in a chauffeur-driven Rolls, owned by a man who had formerly been a clerk in the firm to which I belonged. His father, I have since learned, had been a labouring man.

Suddenly, the bubble burst. I can't remember anyone who claimed they had seen it coming. One day it was all sunshine: the next deluge, darkness and disaster. Even those best placed on the watchtowers of the city, the finance kings and stockbrokers, failed to see the portents and were caught as unprepared as the poor devils who had relied on them for advice and guidance.

Howard Spring, writing in 1945, described this financial debacle in his book 'And Another Thing . . .' (Constable & Co.) and I can do no better than repeat his version of what happened.

> Twenty years after the time of which I write (the first decade of this century), our city (Cardiff), notable now for snug unadventurous security, would see rocket millionaires soaring aloft, throwing off dazzling sparks that many fools rushed to gather, to find their fingers burned and to see the rockets explode and disappear like the pretentious nothingness they were. Great wealth for a few (and for a moment) and deep poverty for many, were to follow upon this poised, comfortable, 'warm' and guinea-guarding moment of which I write. It was to me, who had then left the city and watched the spectacle from afar, of a deeper interest because I had played in the back streets with one of these masters of financial jugglery whose name became known throughout the country before it fizzled out like a firework in a puddle.

I knew Spring's boyhood friend of the back streets at the time when his name 'fizzled out like a firework in a puddle.' He was the promoter of that ill-starred attempt to make a fortune and establish a reputation, the Western Counties Shipping Co. Ltd., which without doubt was the worst calamity suffered by investors in a Cardiff enterprise in the immediate post-war years. He had been a clerk in the accounts department some years before my joining the firm and often came into the office to consult Mr. Annear when the crash seemed imminent. For some years he had prospered on his own (as a ship-owner in a small way he could hardly have done otherwise in the conditions then prevailing) and felt the time had come to launch his big venture. He could not see the clouds just peeping over the horizon. I remember reading his prospectus. It appeared in the national press but was given special prominence in the South Wales newspapers. Like all prospectuses it sounded good. Fortunately for me I had no spare cash at the time (nor for many years afterwards!). As I recall the affair the promoter was unlucky or foolish enough to buy at the height of the post-war boom a fleet of tramp steamers owned by a company on Tyneside, paying in part and mortgaging the balance, the security for the mortgage being the fleet of steamers. With startling suddenness came the slump: one day cargo space was wanted and it seemed only the next day when it was discovered that there was a vast surplus of ships' holds and nothing to put in them. Freight rates plummeted and ships were laid up: those belonging to my company found a cheap resting place in the sandy estuaries of the North Cornwall coast from which their sailing ship forerunners had been launched, and from which they had traded seventy years earlier.

With little or no money coming in and much going out, the Western Counties could not meet its mortgage repayments and probably defaulted even on the interest. The vendors foreclosed, taking back all their ships at their enormously reduced values while retaining the down payment. I have long forgotten the financial details, but this, broadly speaking, was what happened. Of considerably more interest to me than the financial juggling was the effect of the crash on the ambitious entrepreneur and those whom he had duped. I remember him coming into the office at the height of the crisis and nervously asking me whether the boss would see him immediately. I was shocked by the change in his appearance: hollow-eyed and grey of countenance as if he hadn't slept for a week.

In his fall he brought down with him many who deserved better. I suppose most of those whose hopes of making a quick profit sank with the foundering of the Western Counties suffered in silence, ashamed to acknowledge their folly even to their friends, but others, and there were a great many, expressed their chagrin and railed at the author of their misfortune in letters to the Cardiff newspapers. They came from war widows and from miners and steelworkers who had entrusted their wartime savings to this man, having been dazzled by the huge fortunes made out of Cardiff ships and beguiled by the mouth-watering pos-sibilities set out in the prospectus. Those who had blown their surplus wartime earnings on booze and tobacco or provided their wives with two pianos (both in the same small room—a common Cardiff joke in those days) had enjoyed their few years of hard work and better than usual rewards, while the abstemious and thrifty had nothing to show (not even a piano) for their self-denial. I felt much sympathy for all the writers and deeply sorry for those most badly hurt, but they got little comfort from their fellow workers whose attitude was one of derision—'Serves them bloody well right: trying to be bloody capitalists!'

About the same time a similar drama was played out in the office where I worked. A senior clerk had joined with a recently retired Welsh ship's captain from the firm's fleet to buy and run a small tramp steamer, forming a company for the purpose, The P........ Shipping Co. Ltd. (named after a middle-class area of Cardiff) with themselves and their families as the main, possibly the only, shareholders. All went well to begin with; a renumerative charter had taken the ship to a Black Sea port, but by the time it had got there the bubble had burst and, in spite of desperate efforts, a return cargo could not be found, and to return in ballast to this country, where similar ships were being laid up would involve financial ruin. The nice, old, benign and brave ship's captain seemed to accept the threat of ruin with some equanimity—I suppose after a lifetime at sea in a tramp steamer he had learned to behave calmly and show fortitude in times of stress—but the poor clerk, thinking no doubt of his wife and children, became frantic with worry. Daily the position worsened, a crew having to be paid and victualled and no end in sight. I noted with sympathy his deepening despair for he was a decent sort. Then one day I entered the office and saw him smiling. On enquiring of a colleague what had happened to cause such a transformation I was told that the ship had run aground in the Danube delta and would become a total loss. They were saved: the insurance would see to that.

I noted that there were a number of providential strandings of this sort in those days.

Observing with acute wonderment all the daily happenings in this strange new world I had learned a lot about private enterprise. I had been very close to men whose decisions controlled, to some extent, the rise and fall of the coal and shipping empire based at that time at Cardiff Docks on which the prosperity of that city was founded. I say 'to some extent', as while at first they appeared to me to be lords of all they surveyed, I soon discovered that factors outside their control were about to bring ruin to some and desolation to many when overseas customers, seemingly simultaneously, all woke up one morning to find that South Wales steam coal was not indispensable. Price reductions both for coal and freight charges did not stimulate demand: it was not wanted at any price that made exporting worth while. What my employers did not know about exporting coal and importing iron ore and grain was not worth knowing, but it was less expensive to lay up their ships in Devon and Cornish estuaries than trying to use them. In two or three years I had seen both boom and bust. Wartime conditions had made it easy for ship-owners to become very rich and their top employees seemed to share largely in this prosperity, but relatively little trickled down to the senior clerks and book-keepers, still less to the junior clerks, most of whom soon got the sack, having to make way for returning ex-service men in fulfilment of promises made when they joined the Armed Forces. And as these were settling down, some with difficulty, for service in Army,

Navy or Flying Corps had given them a taste for a more active way of life, the leaves were beginning to fall from the trees in the autumn chill that preceded the great depression. Therefore many of those who had been but recently reinstated were soon to join in the great exodus, leaving many a desk unattended. But the clerks were not the greatest sufferers. More poignant was the fate of the ships' crews, men who, during the war, had suffered much hardship and survived great dangers. The engineers and firemen held qualifications that enabled them to compete for shore jobs but the other officers and seamen were left stranded. A common story in Cardiff at that time was that a ship had 'just sailed with every deck officer holding a Master's Certificate and every engineer a Chief Engineer's ticket.'

What happened to the money that was made and not lost again soon afterwards in extravagant living or optimistic investment in companies like the Western Counties and Machine Made Sales?

Towards the end of the 1914-18 War those with money to invest were urged, on grounds of patriotic duty ('We owe it to our lads in the Forces') as well as self-interest to put it in 5% War Loan. Many did so, from war widows to industrial and commercial magnates, among them Cardiff shipowners loaded with easily made profits and insurance moneys in respect of lost ships. And during the depression many held on to the investment—the right time for selling and reinvestment never seemed to arrive. Few who invested in 5% War Loan when issued are still alive, but there are doubtless many still alive to whom it has come by inheritance. It is interesting to consider how a fortune, by 1919 values, of £100,000, enough then to buy a country estate with a 'desirable residence', Home Farm, other farms and cottages or a street of houses in, say, Cardiff, would stand to-day, sixty-five years later, if retained by the family of the original investor.

So far in 1984 the price has ranged between £32 and £37 per £100 nominal stock. Let us put it at £35. This means that what cost £100,000 in 1919 would now be worth no more than £35,000—just enough to buy a farm cottage in need of modernization or a terraced house in a less fashionable part of Cardiff suburbia. Worse than that, in the financial crisis of 1931—investors were persuaded to accept a lower rate of interest and the 5% rate was reduced to 3½% at which it still stands. Patriotism allied with ignorance, innocence or lethargy can be costly. For those who used such sums to buy land the story is very different: their descendants can now claim to belong to the landed gentry!

The two men who controlled, and, in large part, owned that group of companies connected with coal and shipping died half a century ago. According to the rules of the game as played before World War II they played fair. It is only after the social upheavals of the last forty years that their attitudes appear to have been grossly selfish and their general behaviour ludicrously pompous. In their own generation they were much respected as the honours and public appointments heaped upon them so eloquently testify. Yet, over the years, when on the first Sunday after Trinity I have listened to the gospel for the day according to the Book of Common Prayer, my mind has sometimes strayed to a Monday morning scene in Mount Stuart Square, Cardiff, where to my idle fancy I saw descendants of Dives and Lazarus in modern dress. The weekly Board Meetings took place on Monday mornings, a fact known not only to those directly concerned but also to some derelict seamen who waited at the office doors for the departure of the two principal directors for lunch at the Exchange Club across the street. One had a wooden leg, into which the stump was socketed just above where a knee joint had been, due, I assumed, to an accident at sea. As the overfed, over-dressed and over-bejewelled bosses descended the steps these mendicants touched their forelocks in salute and held out their grimy palms for the coin that would enable them to return to the James Street pub, with the wherewithal for further refreshment, while the donors proceeded to their club, there to be waited upon deferentially and, in spite of post-war austerity, fed and wined sumptuously. For, as the gospel story has it, between both parties in the drama 'there is a great gulf fixed.' That gulf has narrowed considerably in the sixty-five years since I witnessed that weekly encounter—at least in this country.

As for me, all the junior clerks who were with the firm when I joined it in 1918 were sacked, myself the only exception, as men returning from the war claimed the jobs promised them on enlistment. In my own department a young Air Force officer took over the private secretarial work for the two principal directors and an Army officer returned later to resume responsibility, under the secretary, for the company work. I was relieved of many very exacting duties and relegated to assisting generally as necessary, mostly as a shorthand-typist. Life became easier for me and the rows fewer. It also became much duller and after five years, against the advice of many and the wishes of the boss, I left of my own accord to take up another job. I was soon to regret that decision, not only because I failed 'to make good' in it and, giving it up after the General Strike of 1926, endured many months without work except casual farm labouring provided by sympathetic relatives, but also because on the whole they were a decent lot in that Cardiff Docks office and, I believe, it remained a firm well worth working for, in spite of everything I have written which might suggest the contrary.

Mr. Annear forgave me for my act of desertion in characteristic manner. On my taking leave of him he handed me a note addressed to Mr. Lear, the well-known Cardiff bookseller, requesting him to provide me with the best Scofield Reference Bible, much esteemed by the Brethren, and to charge the cost to his account. On the fly-leaf he wrote 'To my beloved pupil Arthur Jones, 3rd July 1923. W.P.A. 1 Tim. 4c. 16v. 1 Tim 6c. 12-16vv.'

Part III

Strange Interlude
1923 - 1926

The author when aged 21

Strange Interlude

In which I learn more about men, nothing about women and, unhappily, a lot about myself

Between my five years as a trainee secretary in a shipowners' office at Cardiff Docks (1918-23) and my servitude at rural Llanover which began in February 1927, there is a gap of more than three years, of which I have said nothing beyond mentioning that those years at Llanover had been preceded by some months of farm work. That I had taken up this manual work because I would have remained unemployed without it is also made clear. What I have not previously revealed is the reason for that unemployment and what sort of job had led up to it.

I have mentioned in 'Yes, I was a Yesman' how I left my secure and promising employment under Mr. Annear in that shipowners' office, blessed with his goodwill and much against his wishes—he knew I was making a mistake—but avoided saying what had attracted me away. It was certainly not money, though the new job offered me more money than I had been getting when serving the tycoons. My motives must have been mixed—but they certainly included genuine Christian idealism. Laughable as the confession must appear to sophisticated modern youth I was much influenced by the standards of loyalty, integrity and decency portrayed in Mrs. Craik's 'John Halifax, Gentleman,' a story which I suppose is almost unknown to-day although when I was young it was numbered among the classics.

For a better understanding of my action, it is important to bear in mind that the first decade of this century was an era that came to be known as the age of 'muscular Christianity.' It saw the birth of the Boy Scout movement. Famous cricketers like C. T. Studd and C. B. Fry were held up as examples to aspiring boyhood, the former becoming a Christian missionary and the latter commander of a training ship whereon early rising, cold baths and bare feet on frost encrusted decks and rigging were looked upon as contributing to chastity as well as discipline. 'Sound minds in healthy bodies.'

In 1902, the year of my birth, two young businessmen in London, Church of England in allegiance and evangelical in outlook, together with a few like-minded friends, decided to do something about a problem that was doubtlessly troubling them personally but also troubling society generally. It was a personal problem and a social evil that clergymen and ministers seemed unable or unwilling to tackle and these young men took it upon themselves to break what they termed the 'conspiracy of silence.' The problem was sexual immorality and the evils that stemmed from it—family break-down, illegitimacy, venereal diseases. Illegitimacy, especially among the poor, was seen as the cause of much misery in those far-off days when a common response of a father to an erring, pregnant daughter was to tell her 'Get out and don't come back' and the daughter's response, all too often, was to resort to prostitution to maintain herself and child. There is now little or no shame attached to bastardy and the Welfare State has accepted that the single-parent family is as fully entitled to what benefits are going as any other. There was also much evidence of widespread venereal disease, discussed in parlours in hushed whispers and in saloon bars with defeatist resignation: 'Poor chap, it can happen to anyone!'

In Wales a much respected Swansea doctor, Dr. Rawlings, had bravely tackled the subject in a small book entitled 'The Greatest Evil of our Time,' but his voice was as one crying in a wilderness of indifference—or was the apparent apathy a cloak for bewilderment and fear?

In that climate it was difficult for a parson, in front of a mixed congregation, to speak his mind (that is if he had any clear thoughts on the subject) with, say, the frankness of St. Paul in his letters to the churches. Some 'refined' ladies would be sure to take offence and, head in air, walk out. Only men like the Rev. G. A. Studdert-Kennedy (Woodbine Willie) fresh from the battlefields of France dared to speak plainly in front of both sexes on matters which he knew from bitter experience were troubling many of his hearers.

In this atmosphere of unhealthy ignorance and furtive curiosity, Alfred B. Kent and Evelyn E. Bagnall, with some friends, resolved to form a society having among its objectives sex education for the young (restricted at first to boys only) reasoning that it was 'Better to have a fence at the top of the cliff than an ambulance at the bottom,' a challenge to prostitution which they saw as a demand related industry (on the part of men, of course), the encouragement of the practice of religion (by Bible study, prayer and public worship) and participation in athletics and sport, all in pursuit of the virtue of chastity. Chastity before marriage and fidelity afterwards was held to be not only mandatory for all Christians but by such means attainable.

The idea and ideal caught on and an organization to promote these aims was formed in London and given the name Alliance of Honour.

The word honour reminds me of another concept. The quarterly magazine of the organization had on its cover a knight in armour to indicate a chivalrous attitude to women and girls. I believe it was Abraham Lincoln who said, 'God made woman the weaker vessel but gave her the heavier end of the log to lift.' Courtesy and chivalry towards girls and women were therefore held out to be justly required of all men with pretensions to decency. 'Treat every girl as if she were your own sister!' In matters of sexual behaviour the view taken by these young men was that men dictated the tune and women danced to it. So the remedy for the evils they deplored depended on the behaviour of men.

In a few years the Alliance of Honour became successful in attracting the interest and allegiance of thousands of young men, who enrolled as members at an annual fee of two shillings and sixpence (12½p), all pledged to carry out as best they could the ideals I have mentioned. They received the quarterly journal, formed branches, organized public meetings and distributed books and booklets promoting the aims of the Alliance, some already available but lacking opportunities for sale, others specially written. A host of Bishops and leading Free Churchmen were enrolled as Vice-presidents or Patrons, some of whom were willing to speak at the annual meetings which were held always in London, in large halls such as the Queen's, Kingsway or the Westminster Central, and usually well attended. After a few years the demands on the time and energies of the young founders became too much for voluntary and part-time participation, so Kent and Bagnall forsook their business careers and became paid joint-secretaries. Eventually, the full-time staff in London numbered at least six, supported in the evenings by many voluntary helpers.

In 1923 the growth of the movement was such as to justify devolution in Wales and Scotland, with headquarters in Cardiff and Edinburgh. An office friend had introduced me to the movement a few years earlier and I had become a member. So when, in 1923, a national branch for Wales was formed and a native organizing secretary sought, Welsh-speaking if possible, I applied and was appointed at a conference held at Llandrindod Wells (that home of lost causes!). After six weeks' training in London I returned to Cardiff and opened a two-roomed office at 46, Charles Street, which I later shared with the organizer for Moral Welfare for the Diocese of Llandaff, Miss Mary Weaver, and her colleague, Miss Alice Webb, a former nurse, whose full-time job was to 'rescue' and supervise the care of girls in the diocese who had been raped or otherwise sexually molested—and she was kept busy. This was before a vast army of local authority controlled social workers accepted responsibility for looking after severely deprived and molested children.

A committee, based at Cardiff, nominally supervised my activities but in practice I received my instructions from, and was held accountable to, the Head Office in London. As merely Organizing Secretary I was also made subject to the guidance and advice of an Honorary Secretary, the Honourable John H. Bruce, son of the second Lord Aberdare, whose work in Wales for the Order of St. John of Jerusalem, I was pleased to discover recently, has been recognized by a large structure of questionable architectural merit but of much practical convenience in the church of St. John the Baptist in Cardiff. He was quiet and gentle in manner, somewhat ascetic in appearance and possessed of much natural dignity, but with a capacity for expressing his views forcibly when occasion demanded, especially when he thought the funds of the organization (which he did a lot to collect from his friends) were being squandered. Discovering by a chance meeting at Cardiff Central Station that one of the co-founders, Alfred Kent (who by now described himself as Joint Director), had travelled down from London for a meeting in a First-class compartment with a woman secretary to whom he dictated letters during the journey (the secretary returning on the next train to get them typed), there was a first-class row when John Bruce told him he should travel Third Class and without a secretary, drafting the letters on a pad with a pen or pencil. Kent was much put out, arguing that the time and money had been well spent, but my admiration and sympathy went to the aristocrat who, while travelling First-class between his home near Mountain Ash and Cardiff, would not disdain to go Third-class if someone else was paying. When, as sometimes happened, we went out to lunch together it was always a simple meal, taken usually in Woolworth's first floor restaurant in Queen Street—his choice. (Mine would have been the Kardomah!).

My duties as Organizing Secretary were to keep a register of members for Wales, to oversee the branch secretaries and their collection of members' subscriptions, to appeal to past sympathisers for continued financial support and to seek new ones, to organize public meetings as well as provide speakers for meetings held under the auspices of other organizations, clubs, brotherhoods, etc. The aim was to make the Wales branch self-supporting as soon as possible, but I soon discovered that I was hopeless at wheedling money out of people: if on a first approach they said they could not afford to give (few said they were not in sympathy with the object of the movement) I left it at that, despite the fact that their appearance and that of their home or office suggested they were not lacking in spondulicks. I was incapable of exercising the smallest degree of persuasion. So in my time the Wales branch was always dependent on subsidies from London.

For some meetings I got doctors or other concerned and educated laymen to speak. Clergymen and ministers seemed diffident about tackling the subject even before audiences of men only. Sometimes when a meeting had been arranged and advertised a speaker failed to turn up because of sudden illness or travel difficulties. Given enough notice I could often find a replacement, but sometimes I found I had to do the talking. Listening to others and having read all the many books and booklets published by the organization I felt I knew what needed to be said and I was gratified to find that I had the gift of the gab. So increasingly I spoke in public, young as I was, but never without an expenditure of nervous energy that left me feeling limp for hours afterwards, or unable to sleep if it had been an evening meeting.

I took up this work in July 1923, almost on my 21st birthday. I was full of hope and enthusiasm—and, no doubt, conceit. In 1924 I became aware that I was attempting a thankless task for which I was emotionally and temperamentally unfitted, though as an organizer I think I did well all that was required of me. Still, I soldiered on.

Although supposed to be only an organizing secretary, inevitably young men and older ones came to me seeking help with their sexual problems. For some I could offer some understanding and sympathy and possibly, in a few cases, helpful advice; on too many occasions however, I found myself quite out of my depth. I was too young for what was expected of me and, country born and bred, quite unsophisticated. Homosexuals baffled me completely: until then I hadn't even realized that there were men afflicted with an inordinate desire for sexual congress with other men rather than with women. As an organization we seem to have followed the Pauline dictum, 'One is indeed ashamed even to speak about what such men do in secret . . .' (Moffat's translation). The problem was completely ignored both in our publications and speeches. Possibly the fact that homosexual behaviour was a criminal offence at the time was a sufficient excuse for leaving the subject to officers of the law. So when a middle-aged man in great distress came to the office and tried to tell me about some transgression or transgressions I had no understanding of his problem and, I fear, not much sympathy. I think, now, he was fearing arrest.

101

As sexual problems in those days were pushed to the background in people's consciousness—so often I was told by other serious and responsible men, 'I don't want to think about it!'—I made it one of my earliest tasks to bring home, if I could, to the people of Wales, or those of them willing to listen, that the youth of Wales were no more immune from these temptations than those in our big cities—that I must do something to break the so-called 'conspiracy of silence.' True, a Welsh novelist, Caradoc Evans, was attracting much attention at the time by portraying Welsh rural life as seething with lust and riddled with superstition behind a screen of pious hypocrisy, but his 'My People' and other books were dismissed by religious leaders as the evil works of a man with a poisoned imagination and a stranger to reality.

I therefore produced an eight-page booklet, having on its cover a map of Wales outlined in black and superimposed over it in bold red characters, 'NATIONAL GLORY OR DECAY?' Inside, I gave the quotation from which I had extracted these words. They came from a speech by King George V. in which he had said, 'The foundations of national glory are set in the homes of the people . . .' The Medical Officer of Health for Cardiff was sympathetic and supplied me with facts and figures relating to the incidence of venereal disease in the city and detailing some of its effects, including the number of children born blind there because of venereal infection in the parents. Various other facts and figures were quoted to support the claim that we were trying to tackle not only a moral problem but a social one also, costly in terms of health and happiness as well as money.

Whether my booklet did any good beyond attracting a little extra financial support (but possibly not enough to meet its cost) I am unable to say, but artistically it was said by some to be a nice piece of work!

With growing doubts about the value of the work I was doing and my fitness for the job, a chance encounter on a train threw my mind into even greater confusion. On an autumn night in 1924, when returning from a meeting at Llandrindod Wells, I boarded a Great Western express travelling between Crewe and Cardiff at Craven Arms. There were few passengers and in my compartment there was only one other passenger, a man approaching middle-age, I thought, but he could have been in his mid thirties. His whole appearance—pale complexion, stern and somewhat sad demeanour and his funereal clothing (black suit and tie, with white shirt and starched collar) and the fact that he was not smoking (at a time when almost all men smoked)—suggested to me that here, without doubt, was a Welsh Nonconformist minister. He showed no disposition to read, still less to talk, or even awareness of my presence, but sat slumped in his corner, apparently deep in thought and possibly tired and dispirited. The face had a look about it suggestive of a keen intelligence and a determined character. For some time I read, but finding the book boring and curiosity getting the better of me, I decided to engage the stranger in conversation. The portents were discouraging but, in betting terms, I was willing to put the odds at two to one on his being a parson of sorts and, as such, unlikely to be less than civil.

Then as the train rushed through the black Herefordshire night I poked a lion in the ribs and he woke up snarling. The stranger, resenting the intrusion, was cold and monosyllabic which made me flustered and apologetic and to my apologies I unwittingly added insult by confessing that I thought he was a parson. No, he was not a parson and resented being taken for one. But his speech betrayed that he was Welsh: I had been right on that point. Hesitantly and defensively, I explained that I was engaged full-time in religious work in Wales, hoping that he would accept this as an excuse. Instead, it became the theme of a lecture and a bitter one at that from this unwelcoming, unsmiling stranger.

Although he looked and spoke like a Welsh Nonconformist minister of the sterner sort, the now talkative stranger made it plain that he despised the breed and regarded himself as a person of much greater consequence. His vehement repudiation of any religious interest or connection, combined with his fluent flow of well chosen words, suggesting a background of reading and study, encouraged me to risk a further rebuff by asking him to tell me who he was. He said his name was Mainwaring (in Wales this name is pronounced as spelt), that he was Miners' Agent for the Rhondda area and that he had been attending a Miners' Conference at Blackpool. This was the W. H. Mainwaring who in 1933 became Labour Member of Parliament for Rhondda East and held the seat until 1959. That he had been thoughtful and dispirited was understandable. The miners had had, and were still going through, a very lean time. There was much bitterness among them and in the economic conditions prevailing at that time there was little Mainwaring or any other of their leaders could do about it. Oil was replacing coal as bunker fuel for the shipping fleets of the world and South Wales steam coal was not wanted as it had been in the past. Even worse times were to follow: the long and bitter miners' strike of 1926 was less than two years away.

For the work in which I was engaged Mainwaring had no good word. I was wasting my time and if I had any talents as well as a wish to serve the people of Wales I should give up trying to change their ways by moral education and religious enthusiasm and take up the cause of social justice. My abilities, such as they were, were being misdirected. I was peddling opium: what his miners and their families needed could be summed up in one word, 'Bread.' 'Just bread,' he added. Not the 'Bread of Heaven' about which miners and others sang at football matches at Cardiff Arms Park before invoking damnation on the visiting side, but just bread, baker's bread.

His attack on my religious beliefs and the work I was doing was so unexpected, so bitter and pressed home so eloquently and devastatingly, that I had no defence to offer but listened attentively, almost spell-bound, as he expounded the principles of Marxist philosophy, which he plainly regarded as a panacea for all the ills of society. I learned later that he had been a college lecturer in economics before becoming a miners' leader. No lesson at school, no lecture in public hall, on radio or television has made such a lasting impression on me as that delivered to me privately in that express train on that autumn night more than sixty years ago. It has affected my thinking on religious, political and social issues ever since. I suppose that what he did was to make me even more thoughtful, enquiring and critical—no bad thing for a young man of twenty-two.

But to be told by a man of his age, learning, experience and authority that my daily work was a waste of time and talent, that the miners he served had no need of, or use for what I was doing, was depressing and unsettling. I had begun to have such doubts without this diatribe and I was much discouraged. But other work was becoming increasingly difficult to find and I resolved to press on.

Before leaving the subject of Mr. Mainwaring's tirade, I think I should mention his defence of the miners as men, real men, with strong muscles, red blood in their veins yet men of principle, loyal in comrade-ship and having no small streak of heroism in their nature. I didn't demur, in fact he gave me little chance to say anything, and on looking back I'm sure he regarded me as a product of Cardiff suburbia, whose denizens were thought to despise the 'men from the valleys' who came to Cardiff just to see football and get drunk. He did not know that I, too, was from the valleys having spent my first sixteen years among miners, railwaymen, tinplate workers and small farmers.

My worst troubles as organizing secretary arose from what we were pleased to call 'Mass Meetings'—sometimes the attendance hardly justified the adjective—that I was required to arrange in the towns and larger villages of South Wales and, when feasible, mid-Wales. (North Wales remained always outside the range of our Cardiff-based activities). Thus in the winters of 1924-25 and 1925-26 I organized meetings in Cardiff, Newport, Swansea, Llanelli, Barry and Penarth, and in various towns in the Rhondda. The speakers were almost always imported from England, but a Dr. Williams, Principal Medical Officer at the Welsh Board of Health, occasionally responded to my invitation to address our larger meetings and his authoritative approach and gentle and persuasive manner always met with a respectful response.

By now a Women's Section had been formed, but it was merely educational in scope, offering books and booklets on the sexual problems of the young and lectures to selected audiences of women as well as at the so-called Mass Meetings for women and girls for which I obtained speakers from London, notably a Lady Nott-Bower and a woman doctor who had made a name for herself as a writer on the subject. Women were not invited to become members: it was just an auxiliary section.

Attendance at the Mass Meetings would have been small but for a sugaring of the pill. The society had got hold of an American film, 'The Gift of Life,' which showed the process of reproduction, beginning with the simple amoeba and then going on to plant life, fishes and mammals, all in three reels. A fourth reel dealt with human reproduction—at least the woman's part: I assume it was not thought proper to portray the man's part or it might have been deemed merely incidental!

A free film show with a titled lady to address the meeting was an attraction everywhere sixty years ago before radio and television became commonplace and I had no trouble in filling the largest halls for the afternoon meetings for women. The men's evening meetings were hardly less well attended. So booking a suitable hall, I had to arrange for a speaker, chairman, pianist or organist, stewards and, where no projection equipment was installed, to hire projector, fireproof portable projection chamber, a large screen and the services of a projectionist, which I did from a firm of film distributors in Cardiff, the Walturdaw Company. The scope for something to go disastrously wrong was, as I was to discover, immense.

In Cardiff it did so. First, I had to satisfy the Chief Constable that the film was truly in the non-inflammable category and, quite rightly, he was not satisfied until I produced a strip and he had set a match to it. He was able to get it to burn but only steadily and without flaring, so it was passed, albeit a bit reluctantly. Thus I was able to use it in the Cory Hall which did not cater for cinema shows. Here I was up against another difficulty: the clear glass windows were without blinds so for the two afternoon women's meetings I had to buy and fix large sheets of brown paper to keep out the light.

The first afternoon meeting for women, which was packed to the doors, passed off well. That night the large hall was full again for the first of the two men's meetings. As usual, it began with a hymn, 'Fight the Good Fight,' or 'Soldiers of Christ, arise,' followed by the 'Chairman's Remarks' (seldom less than a short speech whatever time restrictions I tried to apply) and, according to the programme, the first three reels of film. That night disaster struck. We had not got far with the second or third reel when a loud explosion in the vestibule, where the portable projection chamber had been set up, stopped the show. Although it was heard throughout the hall there was no panic. I rushed in the darkness to find out what had happened and discovered that a large transformer (a roughish contraption of wire coils on a metal frame), used to convert the mains current to the voltage required for the projector, had shorted, one of the coils having sagged and come into contact with the frame. Lights were put on and I went on to the platform to explain what had happened, promising to do my best to get another transformer and calling on the speaker, who was the Dr. Williams already mentioned, to give his address. The projectionist told me that there was a similar transformer at the Welsh Medical School just up the road. So running there I confirmed from a caretaker that this was true but he refused (and I didn't blame him) to lend it. Dr. Williams was still speaking when I got back to the Cory Hall and it was my sorry task as soon as he had finished to go on to the platform again and apologise for my failure but promising to have the transformer repaired in time for the meetings on the following day, so that if any present wanted to see the rest of the film, they would be able to do so (all being well!) on the following night; the collection would be taken and the closing hymn sung. The collection was taken but it was never enough to cover the cost of these meetings, however large the attendance. Though we did not pay headquarters for the hire of the film nor the speakers for their services (some, even when travelling from a distance, also waived their expenses) the cost of hiring the projector and the services of an operator was heavy. It was that night, too, that passing the caretaker's cubby hole in the vestibule, I caught sight of the caretaker helping himself to handfuls of coins from the collection plates I had left in his care! For one night I had, I felt, had more than enough.

But my troubles were not over. Dr. Williams came to me and said that my invitation to those present to return the following night had put him in a quandary: he had only one speech for the occasion and nobody would wish to hear it twice, so would I get someone else? Fortunately I was able to do so and the two meetings on the following day passed off without mishap, though by now my nerves were on edge. Going twice on to that platform before a large audience to explain and apologise (and I was only twenty-two) was not easy, though the audience was sympathetic and understanding.

In the early spring of 1926 we held similar meetings in the Rhondda. I remember those at Porth and Treorchy only vaguely—but the memory of the one at Ferndale haunted me for years and I can still recall vividly all that happened. In the mining valleys we held such meetings in the Miners' Welfare Halls which, being already equipped for cinematograph shows, spared us the expense, trouble and hazards we had experienced at Cardiff and elsewhere. Times were hard in the Rhondda and the free film show attracted large audiences of men only and women only. So the large hall at Ferndale was filled almost to capacity by men, mostly miners, that night in March. The programme was exactly the same as that at Cardiff and elsewhere. The chairman at Ferndale was either a local clergyman or a layman of some distinction, possibly a local magistrate: I've forgotten but, whoever he was, he wasn't much use as things turned out.

To my dismay, Head Office had sent down as speaker not Alfred Kent, as I had hoped, but his co-founder, Evelyn Bagnall. Kent, who usually came, was a charismatic figure, rather Pickwickian in appearance, with a confident platform manner and, for these large meetings, a set, unvarying speech which he delivered with histrionic effect, playing on his audiences' feelings as on a stringed instrument, the whispered joke delivered confidentially, followed sharply by the fierce denunciation or urgent, persuasive appeal. He was a charmer and always went down well. He was particularly good at the rhetorical question and declamatory answer. At one point in his speech he would stutter, as if searching for just the right word and then, suddenly smiling, he would discover it. He knew at what point to expect the first applause and the first laugh and was able to assess how he was doing by the degree of warmth expressed in those early responses. It all sounded spontaneous and was extremely effective when heard for the first time. But hearing it all for, say, the fifth time and knowing at any moment precisely what oratorical trick came next, the effect on me was somehow somewhat nauseating. Naturally, I began to suspect Kent of being a pious hypocrite; but I would be wrong: he knew what his hearers wanted to hear and saw no reason to change his style or his words.

But poor Evelyn Bagnall, with his set speech had difficulty in getting his message across in any gathering of, say, more than fifty, however friendlily disposed. He was about fifty, of medium height and build, a dapper type of man, and he came to poverty-stricken Ferndale and stood before that crowd of mufflered, shabbily dressed men, clad like a London shop-walker (a breed now extinct), with a winged, butterfly-type collar, a silky cravat, a neat dark grey suit, a white lining edging his waistcoat and, I believe, light coloured spats, his greying hair brushed carefully back from his thin, sallow and rather unhappy face. He suffered always from dyspepsia and in those days was never without charcoal biscuits. I felt sorry for him and before that night was out my heart ached for him, yet, as we never seemed to be on the same wavelength, he irritated me greatly. He was a good man, but in the wrong job and, as I was discovering for myself, so was I.

The meeting began quietly enough. The opening hymn was sung with the verve one could expect of Rhondda men, the chairman did his stuff, the first three reels of film were shown and received in silence. The lights went up and Mr. Bagnall walked on to the stage to deliver his address. He had not uttered more than a few sentences when I sensed trouble brewing. Whether it was his public school accent which might have given those present a feeling that they were being 'talked down to' or his somewhat foppish appearance, or both, I don't know, but there was a restlessness in that crowded hall that I had not previously known, a general murmur which made it difficult for those even half way back to hear the speaker (there was no public address system in those days). He was proceeding as usual, smiling and gesticulating when the text called for it, when someone in the audience blew a 'raspberry.' Loud and appreciative laughter! Still, Mr. Bagnall continued as if nothing untoward was happening. Then more 'raspberries' and some belching. Things were getting out of hand and, knowing these chaps (or rather others like them in my native village) I felt something must be done. I had seen a policeman outside the doors as the men streamed in, a burly officer of the Glamorgan County Police. He was still there. I told him things threatened to get rough inside the hall—could he do anything about it? He said no, but would have a look. He sauntered in to the corridor that ran down one side of the hall and, opening two or three swing doors a couple of inches, peeped through. It was enough to show some men sitting near that there was a police presence. (Since the recent year-long miners' strike I have learned that a police presence provokes violence rather than prevents it!). I went into the hall again. There was Mr. Bagnall struggling to go on with his speech but I was sure that the noise was such as to make him inaudible even to those in the front rows. 'Raspberries' and belches had now given place to groans and shouts of disapprobation. Soon, I feared, chairs would be thrown.

Without premeditation, acting only on instinct stimulated by anger, I ran up the steps to the stage and stood by Mr. Bagnall—a move which so surprised the groaners and shouters as to produce relative quiet. Mr. Bagnall also stopped. And in that silence I said—God knows where I got it from as it was a phrase I had heard only occasionally and had probably never used it myself or had need to—'Chwarae teg, boys!' (Fair play, boys!). With that the silence became complete, enabling me, in my 'valleys' accent, to appeal to them to give the speaker from London a fair hearing and threaten that if they didn't behave they wouldn't see the last part of the film. The 'boys' I was scolding had, I think, an average age at least double my own but they responded perfectly, allowing Mr. Bagnall to finish his speech if not in respectful silence, at least silence unbroken even by a whisper. At all these meetings, before the last reel (that dealing with human reproduction) was shown, the 139th psalm was read. It was so on this occasion: it was read well and received reverently. The last reel was shown and the last hymn sung as if everything had been orderly from the beginning.

That meeting, followed, after a very late return home by train to Barry, by a sleepless night, marked the end for me. I had had enough and became very depressed. I resolved to give up the job as soon as possible. But no sooner had I made this resolve than the prolonged miners' strike of 1926 began, accompanied, at the beginning, by the short-lived General Strike. Immediately, my father, an engineer in a Barry ship-repairing firm, was sacked together with all his workmates. The firm had been teetering on the edge of solvency for some time and this strike finished it. My father remained out of work for months and my pay was needed to keep the family afloat, and though I longed to be free of any further obligation to organize meetings, collect funds and encourage branch secretaries, I had to continue at my now hated work for the whole of that dreary summer. In late August or early September my father found new employment with the Barry Railway and with him again earning I was free to resign. I did so and became unemployed. I had not expected otherwise as in the months following the Ferndale meeting I had seen only one job advertised for which I felt qualified and that I failed to get. But I was desperate, feeling that if I did not get out I would go dotty, if I were not dotty already.

Apart from my own experience, the experience of my jobless friends and others went to confirm in my mind that in giving up paid employment at such a time I was behaving very foolishly and some told me so. An illustration: some weeks earlier, on approaching Cardiff Central Station for my nightly journey home I had been stopped by a well-dressed young man of about my own age who asked if I could give him a shilling or two to get back home to Swansea. He told me he was an out-of-work clerk and had come up to Cardiff to look for work—there was nothing for him at Swansea. Rather unkindly, perhaps, I said to him 'Why not pawn your watch?' (This is what I would have done rather than resort to begging in the street). He had a gold or gold finished watch chain across his waistcoat. He pulled out the ends: there was no watch. He was wearing the chain to keep up appearances. In those days clerks had to avoid any suggestion of scruffiness. Gentility was all. After this, though hard-up myself, I felt I had to help him on his way. Why, it might be asked, did he not hitch-hike back to Swansea? He would not have thought of it, nor would I. There were few cars and hitch-hiking had not become a recognized form of travel for the young. So I knew what I might be letting myself in for.

For the first few weeks I continued to go to the public library, there taking my turn at the newspaper stands with smelly old men, some peering through magnifying glasses, all trying to discover a consensus on the day's winners. I was willing to tackle any job anywhere as my meagre savings were rapidly running out, but still there was nothing offering. I was not entitled to the 'dole' which, for a single man, was, I think, fifteen shillings a week, as I had given up my job voluntarily. To qualify I had to be sacked for incompetence, disobedience or disgraceful conduct of some kind and I could not imagine how that could be reconciled with the testimonial I had been given by London headquarters which was essential for securing further employment in any position of trust. (Later, I discovered that I did not qualify for work in the Post Office at Christmas, on which I had counted, as although I was over eighteen priority was given to men who had served in the Forces during the 1914-18 War and as more than enough came forward this meant in 1926 that no one under twenty-six stood a chance.)

The only opening I could discover was that offered by the Canadian Government, who provided passage to Canada and a guarantee of farm employment there to young men who were fit, had some experience of farming and were able to pay £10. Bodily I was still fit; as a boy I had worked on farms and I felt I could borrow £10. My maternal grandfather, albeit a bit reluctantly, confirmed in writing that I had some experience of farming and was of good character. I thus became an approved candidate for emigration and went back to the farms at Machen and Rhiwderin I had left in 1918, as much to harden myself for the life on the prairies as to learn some more about farming. So back to the cabbage cutting, mangold pulling and pulping, chaff cutting, dung carting and spreading that I had left thankfully behind me eight years earlier, between school and my first job. To these skills (if such they be), I added a new one: hedge-laying in which my grandfather was an expert. I realized that competence at hedge-laying, as was the case with much else I was doing on these Welsh farms, would not be of the slightest use in Canada, but I had the sense to realise that an ability to use tools competently—axe, bill-hook, brushing hook, fork, spade and so on—could not fail to be of some use in Canada or elsewhere. (Elsewhere, fifty years later in my retirement, has been the orchard in Kent belonging to my son-in-law and daughter, where many hours of hedge trimming and hedge-laying have given me enormous satisfaction).

Dung carting from the midden was a pleasurable experience, and I looked forward when getting up in the morning to a day in which I had NOT to listen futilely to any miserable confidences, write letters, cajole unwilling donors for money or organize meetings. Instead, after the farmhouse breakfast of home-cured bacon and eggs, with home-baked bread, washed down with the weakest of tea, to harness the docile mare and shunt her into the cart, and pitch forkfuls of dung, thence to the field, there to deposit it in well-spaced heaps for spreading later, all in the open air and in that mid-winter often in crisp frosty air. That and hedge-laying in the hill-side fields at Machen, overlooking a pleasant rural section of the Rhymney valley, through which three railways ran, all converging below me, with trains, mostly coal-bearing, passing every few minutes, the main road weaving between the railways, itself carrying a few cars, a baker's van but still with many horse-drawn vehicles—that was bliss indeed, so much so, that I sometimes found myself singing (out of tune, I fear, but I had only the old mare as audience) snatches from favourite hymns and songs. Back to the farmhouse for dinner, the afternoon then spent on some other task, then back to tea of home-made cakes and jam, also always home-made with fruits grown on the farm.

111

Those long winter evenings in the warm farmhouse kitchen after a day in the open air or barn also helped to reduce the nervous tension within me. There, night after night, I sat reading at the kitchen table in the light of an oil lamp. 'Dad,' our grandfather, and Gwyn, my brother would be similarly engaged, while Violet Beecham, the young, pretty and hard-working maid, with the sharp tongue when provoked, sat, cat in lap, before the blazing fire, content just to rest, while under the table the two sheep dogs slept and occasionally snored. Dad's favourite reading was the 'Western Mail' and 'Farm, Field and Fireside,' a weekly journal. From time to time, coming across a news item or story which he thought might be of some interest to 'Mam,' our grandmother, he would tell her in Welsh of his discovery which more often than not led to her asking him to read it to her as she sewed or darned. I, too, listened as he read in English but Mam's comments or any discussion between them was always in Welsh, which I failed to understand, but Gwyn, then living permanently on the farm, could understand and sometimes translated for my benefit.

The day ended with a snack of Mam's Caerphilly cheese and her home-baked bread with a glass of milk or whey or beer and early to bed. This was, in truth, the good life. No better therapy could have been devised for one in my condition and as the weeks passed my gloom and depression evaporated.

I was not paid: board and lodging was enough and probably as much as I was worth, anyway, and I have never ceased to be grateful to my grandparents, who, in the harsh conditions for hill farmers in Wales were having a lean time. Colour returned to my cheeks and my muscles regained their strength. I became increasingly confident that a Canadian farmer would find me almost as useful as I was willing. But, as I have reported in 'His Lordship's Obedient Servant,' my mother, desperate to save me from such folly, intervened by pressing me to apply for the vacancy advertised in the 'Western Mail' for a clerk in the Llanover Estate Office and I only got to Canada forty-five years later when returning from Montreal by sea after a holiday marking my retirement.

The organization for which I had worked so unsparingly did not survive the Second World War. The change of attitude that later became recognized as the 'permissive society' was already stirring in the womb. Thus it came about that the standards that I with other earnest and idealistic young men sought to uphold—courtesy, chivalry, self-discipline, 'chastity before marriage and fidelity after marriage'—if one dares mention them in supposedly polite company, are as likely as not to evoke the sort of smile given by the kindly disposed to the simple minded or even incredulous laughter, no less in Wales, that former bastion of Puritanism, than over the border.

Part IV

His Lordship's Obedient Servant
1927 - 1934

Major General Lord Treowen, C.B., C.M.G. A portrait painted by Sir William
Llewellyn

Vassals and Villeins

In 1926, following the General Strike and during the prolonged miners' strike, I became unemployed. After some months of idleness, shared with hundreds of other young South Walians similarly or better qualified, all milling around for the few office jobs occasionally advertised, I decided to seek work and fortune, as many of my friends and acquaintances were doing, in the New World. Without money the U.S.A. was barred to me but for £10 I could go to Canada as an assisted emigrant, subject to my being fit for, and willing to undertake, farm work. I applied, was approved and spent the winter of 1926-27 in unpaid farm work by way of training and as a hardening process. While I was thus engaged, my mother saw a tiny advertisement in the 'Western Mail' for a clerk in the Llanover Estate Office near Abergavenny in Gwent and pressed me to apply. I did so and, faced with much competition, was surprised to find myself appointed. My success was possibly due to the fact that, in addition to my secretarial training, I could offer my farming background as an extra qualification, as my work on the Estate would relate chiefly to farms, farmers and farming.

My pay was to be fifty-five shillings a week payable monthly. My lodgings there with Mrs. Pedr James were to cost me thirty shillings a week if I went home to Barry over Saturday night, otherwise her charge was thirty-five shillings a week, payable weekly. By now I was almost penniless so I had to borrow to see me through to that first pay-day and a friend, lending me £10, did just that.

Looking back, I can't decide whether it was ill-luck, good-luck or divine intervention (in response to my mother's fears) that switched me from the adventurous and possibly dangerous course on which I was bound, to one that was too comfortably safe, deadly boring, and, for a young man, spirit sapping. I had not been in my new job more than a few weeks before feeling that I had taken a wrong turning. I had landed myself in a sort of open prison, from which in those days of deep depression and rising unemployment, escape seemed impossible. Although I applied surreptitiously for other jobs, I failed to get one. At twenty-four, physically fit and temperamentally restless, I was now confined to a sedentary way of life so stifling and enervating as to be almost unendurable—made no more acceptable by the congratulations of those who thought I had been lucky! The more enterprising of the young people in the village and from the surrounding farms got away, I noticed, as soon as school-days were over.

Between my comfortable lodgings with Mrs. James and the Estate Office door was a walk that could be covered in less than two minutes unless I dawdled. This, in the dark evenings of winter, was my only exercise for five of the seven days of the week, as there was nothing in the village or near it to encourage me to go out in the dark. I do remember, however, on some clear frosty nights when the moon was full, taking long walks in the lanes, the only sounds accompanying my footfalls being the rumble of a distant train, the hooting of an owl and the barking of farm dogs. The farmers and villagers who worked hard all day in the open air and could only be lured from their firesides at night for the most urgent of reasons would have concluded that I was either crazy or up to no good had I been seen on these nocturnal jaunts. Only poachers after Lord Treowen's rabbits and pheasants and his Lordship's gamekeepers after poachers would naturally be out and about on moonlit nights.

For a brief spell I got up early and, in football shorts, ran a mile or two along the canal bank but this extraordinary behaviour only served to confirm that the new Estate Clerk was 'not all there.' (Jogging as a recognized form of exercise was still forty years away). In that first summer of 1927 I got together a local football team and, without much difficulty, was able to find a flat playing field and a convenient changing room in the Estate Yard near it. Of that changing room I will have more to say later. Playing in the team myself, I was able to obtain some pleasurable exercise at least in winter.

Hardly less irksome for me than the physical restrictions were the restraints upon behaviour arising from social, moral and religious attitudes. Socially, my status could have been defined by reference to Garnier's 'Land Agency' (Second Edition 1899), an authoritative introduction to the profession of a Land Agent. At Llanover, along with the surveyor, book-keeper and junior clerk in the office and the forty or so manual workers—carpenters, masons, bricklayers, plumbers, painters, sawyer, carters, quarrymen and so on—I was subordinate to the sub-agent. Garnier's specification for a sub-agent reads . . . 'the sort of person required for a sub-agent is not a gentleman, but one who has a good stock of empirical knowledge picked up by actual labour; and will carry out orders and not try to improve upon them. A man with a gentleman's education would find the subordinate office too irksome . . .'

The sub-agent at Llanover fitted this description exactly. He was a Yorkshireman who had some difficulty in disguising the fact that he looked upon the Welsh as a foreign race—as, indeed, to him they were. They displayed little interest in cricket and he formed and captained a Llanover team. They neglected the parish church in favour of their Nonconformist chapels and he was a church-warden. Later, I was to learn that enthusiasm for cricket and lay office of some sort in the Anglican church were generally accepted, in England at least, as reliable credentials when applying for employment on the large private estates. I lacked both qualifications, but in Wales, and especially at Llanover, these deficiencies didn't seem to count as much as they did over the border. Helpful, but not essential! As a subordinate, therefore, of one who was NOT a gentleman (cricket captaincy and churchwardenship notwithstanding) and not required to be one, I was something less than a non-gentleman and it would do me no good to pretend otherwise. I soon found my place and came to accept that I was slotted into a category only slightly above that of the skilled tradesmen and slightly below that of the more prosperous valley farmers and so was deemed by common understanding to be on the school teacher/hill farmer rung of the social ladder. Had I shown any disposition to climb higher or, by consorting too freely with those markedly inferior in social status, slipped a rung or two lower, the result would have been overt disapproval and some degree of ostracism.

My neighbours were honest and hardworking. Parents were dutiful to their children and, with few exceptions, homes were well kept in spite of what would now be regarded as degrading poverty. In sexual matters, too, standards were high but adherence, at best, patchy.

One warm summer's day Lord Treowen, while walking on his land by the waters of the river Usk, was horrified to discover the children of his sub-agent with some friends, boys and girls, bathing together. He ordered them out of the water and commanded them not to repeat the offence. The girls were covered from shoulders to above the knees with the long bathing 'costumes' of those days and the boys at least adequately covered, but in his eyes it was indecent and many in the village and on the Estate concurred.

There were many 'shot-gun' marriages and I was impressed by the long memories retained by my landlady in these matters. She and others, long resident in the area could, and did, point out to me couples who had transgressed in this way more than twenty years earlier.

In religion, conformity was all. Not to the parish church, which had recently ceased to be a part of the Church of England and become instead an outpost of the Church in Wales, for it was poorly attended, but to Nonconformist Puritanism. Its influence was seen in the honesty and integrity of most of those who followed its tenets—and they formed the majority among us—and in their acceptance of what has since become known as the Protestant work ethic (although there are many today who do not regard this as an unqualified virtue). What most rankled within me was their Sabbatarianism. The proper degree of Sunday observance, I felt, should be left to one's conscience. It was all right for those working on the land for six days of the week to appreciate and enjoy rest and attendance at chapel on Sunday—but what about me, stuck in an office for five and a half days of the week and bursting with energy at the short week-end? One summer Sunday evening after my landlord, Pedr James, and his kindly wife had left for chapel I thought I would do them a good turn and, taking a hoe, began weeding their very large vegetable garden. I had been at it for only a few minutes when a passing group of chapel-goers shouted at me to put away the tool and behave like a Christian! Shocked, I still carried on hoeing and what I received from Pedr James was not gratitude but a rebuke. A few years later, being then married and living at No. 10 Tre Elidyr, where I had a large garden, I was often tempted to work in the garden on Sundays but, intimidated by local opinion, did so only when I thought I was not observed. I was not the only coward there. Jack Griffiths, the Estate plumber, lived next door. One bright summer Sunday afternoon I saw him, hands in pockets, inspecting his garden and, guessing that he was itching to do some work in it, I said, 'I see you don't do any work in your garden on Sundays, Jack.' 'Oh yes I do,' he replied and added, 'I looks up the road and I looks down the road and if I don't see anybody coming I snatches at a few weeds.'

The restriction of my new way of life in a job that demanded little of me and offered no scope for initiative, accounts for the fact that I did not realise at the time my good fortune to be living in one of the loveliest parts of Wales and, from a cultural point of view, a place of exceptional interest. I was witnessing, although I did not know it, the end of an era.

The main fact distinguishing Llanover from other villages in Gwent was that for about a century it had been, and still was, an island of Welsh culture in an encroaching sea of Englishness. Its defences were giving way in my time and I am sure that the waves of televised Anglo-American pop culture in recent decades have almost wholly washed away all traces of that Welsh bastion of fifty years ago. It owed its unique Welshness to the fact that throughout almost the whole of the 19th century it had been the home of a renowned and influential Welsh

Painting by Lady Llanover of Welsh girl in the costume of Pembrokeshire
Reproduced by permission of the National Library of Wales

Painting by Lady Llanover of Welsh girl in the costume of part of Gwent

Reproduced by permission of the National Library of Wales

patriot, Lady Llanover. Born there in 1802, daughter of one Benjamin Waddington, her maiden name does not suggest a Welsh ancestry, but from a biographical dictionary I learn that she was descended 'in a direct line from the Royal House of Plantagenet as well as from the ancient royal and noble families of Wales.' Be that as it may, she was a woman of exceptional intelligence and energy and directed both gifts to the promotion and perpetuation of Welsh literature, speech, poetry, song and even dance. As regards the last, she discovered and revived a Welsh folk dance, still known as the Llanover reel. She founded the Welsh Manuscript Society. She was a talented painter and her works include pictures showing women dressed in the costumes worn in different parts of Wales, which have been reproduced in a series of postcards by the National Library of Wales. Her zeal in these matters, especially in connection with the National Eisteddfod and local eisteddfodau, earned her the bardic title Gwenynen Gwent (the Bee of Gwent)—but whether that was because of the bee's ability to sting or its capacity to produce honey, I'm not sure! It thus followed that all her employees at Llanover were required to speak Welsh. In 1927 her harpist, Gruffydd, had been dead many years but his daughter, Mrs. Gruffydd Roberts, was still living there and, although blind, playing her father's harp. Pedr James, my landlord at 1 Tre Elidyr, had been a penillion singer and his harp, then silent, stood in a corner of my sitting room. Reuben Lewis, the house carpenter at the Mansion where he employed his manual skills as a cabinet maker, then aged, but still active bodily and mentally, was also a minor poet and had earned the bardic title Madoc Môn, having been born and brought up in Anglesey, in Welsh Môn.

That the Welsh cultural pattern, so firmly established by Lady Llanover in her lifetime, was still affecting behaviour there thirty-one years after her death, was brought home to me on a curious and memorable occasion in the summer of 1927. As mentioned earlier, I had got together a Llanover football team and found a good playing field almost adjoining the Estate Yard and persuaded the sub-agent to allow us the use of a large room in the yard as a changing room and meeting place. It meant asking Mr. Williams, the recently retired Estate Foreman whose office it had been, to clear out his desk there. In doing so he came across a piece of sheet music that some years earlier had been a test piece in a local eisteddfod, a quartet for male voices, in which he had taken part. Instead of throwing it away with the other rubbish, he brought it into the Estate Office to show David Griffiths, the book-keeper. 'How does it go, Mr. Williams?' asked Griffiths. 'I can't remember,' replied Mr. Williams and added, 'Let's try it!' And try it they did, old Mr. Williams in his quivering bass and Griffiths in his firm and tuneful tenor. Thus I first heard and was captivated by 'Myfanwy,' that enchanting Welsh song, which has since become one of the most requested items wherever Welsh male voice choirs sing. First, they hummed the melody. They then sang it in Welsh, to the plaudits of Bert Evans, the estate architect and surveyor, and myself. Evans was then asked to contribute his baritone and did so willingly. The result was even more impressive. The three then pressed me to join in as second bass. I protested but my excuses—tone deafness and inability to read music (a lack which I have since remedied)—were not accepted and after Griffiths had rehearsed me carefully and declared the result satisfactory, I made the fourth member of the quartet. And a good time was had by all, before Griffiths returned to his ledger, Evans to his drawing board and I to my typewriter. I have since asked myself whether that impromptu concert in an office during working hours could have taken place in any other part of the British Isles for it seems to me that the scene captured the essence of something which was typically Welsh.

With all her activities in and for Wales, Lady Llanover was also a leading figure in London society, especially in those circles devoted to the encouragement of literature and the arts. In 1823 she married Benjamin Hall, who later became a Member of Parliament and, rising to high office in the Government, was responsible, as First Commissioner of Works, for choosing, installing and unwittingly naming the big bell in the clock tower of the Palace of Westminster. More than 120 years later Big Ben still announces the hour on British radio and television. Such was the name by which the tall and handsome Sir Benjamin Hall was affectionately known by his friends in Parliament. He was created a baron in 1859 and, dying in 1867, aged 65, was buried at Llanover.

I had been in the Estate Office some weeks when in came an elderly man whose appearance and manner caught and held my attention. He was tall and handsome. He was also erect, even soldierly, in his bearing and he conducted his business with the sub-agent, who was not merely dwarfed but in a curious way seemingly humbled by this visitor with assurance and dignity lightened by a ready smile. On his leaving I turned to David Griffiths and asked, 'Who was that?' Instead of answering he asked me to tell him why I was interested. I must have said something on the lines that the visitor had looked every inch an aristocrat. He had been expecting some such comment and smiled as he said, 'Strange that you should have said that!' He then told me this story. The man I had seen was a retired coachman living in a cottage on the Estate. He had been born in the middle of last century, the illegitimate son of a widow in one of the four lodges that guarded the entrances to the Park and Mansion. It had been Lord Llanover's custom, when any lodge-keeper died or otherwise departed, to fill the vacancy, in his charity, with a deserving widow. Servants, other employees and tenants, however, saw that the widows chosen were relatively young and among themselves questioned whether charity was the sole consideration in their selection. But in spite of intense interest, natural in such a closed community, the poor mother never revealed the identity of the child's father. He grew up into a handsome lad, was given employment in his Lordship's stables and eventually became head coachman. By this time those old enough to remember remarked on the striking resemblance exhibited by the young coachman to Lord Llanover, then many years deceased. But had Lord Llanover transgressed in this way, which on the evidence is more than likely, he would have done no more than was commonly regarded as exercising the rightful privilege of a feudal landowner.

Lady Llanover died in 1896, aged 93, leaving only one daughter, two sons having predeceased her husband. The daughter, the Honourable Mrs. Herbert, ruled at Llanover in her stead and loyally maintained the Welsh traditions instituted by her mother. When, in 1927, I went to Llanover Mrs. Herbert had been dead for some thirteen years. She was not remembered with affection: she had used her powers over her many servants, indoors and out, unkindly and unwisely, even despotically. It seemed that she had been a tyrant and inquisitor, setting servant against servant. But not all her orders were fully obeyed.

Her butler was commanded to sleep at the Mansion, never with his wife in her cottage in the village; and this ordinance applied to every night of the year. To what extent it was disobeyed was never known, but gamekeepers out at night from time to time reported to their friends that in the darkness they had seen a figure, resembling the butler, hurrying across the Park; someone, they were sure, not interested in pheasants or rabbits. And the butler did leave a daughter with whom, in summer, I played tennis.

Mrs. Herbert's husband had predeceased her by many years. He had been a member of a family who had owned lands in Monmouthshire for many generations—they claimed for centuries—and his Estate at

Llanarth was only six miles away. At Llanover, so legend had it, he put up with his wife's rule, as did everyone else. So in 1927 I could count myself to be luckier than those who had preceded me some twenty years earlier. Their eldest son, Ivor John Caradoc Herbert, who became Lord Treowen in 1917 was said to be wise and fair, even if a bit of a martinet, which was only natural in a soldier whose ancestors had fought at Agincourt and in the Wars of the Roses!

We saw little of him in the Estate Office as, apart from his trips abroad (always on official business, never for pleasure) he also had his paternally descended Estate at Llanarth and his town home in Mayfair. It was with some surprise, therefore, that in the summer of 1928 I was summoned by the Estate Agent to go to his Lordship's study immediately as he wished to make me his private secretary and I was to begin work at once.

This appointment can truly be said to have come out of the blue: I had aimed at another bird and had brought down this one as well as the other of which I will speak later. I owe the success of this feat to two men, whose origins, education and characters could hardly be more disparate. First the agent to the Estates who had appointed me in the first place, Leslie R. Pym, who must have spoken so well of me that Lord Treowen did not consider it necessary to interview me—until then I had been to him merely a new face in the office. Leslie Pym seems to me now, in retrospect, a perfect model of the upper-class Englishman—and none the worse for that. He claimed descent from John Pym, who, with John Hampden, took the side of Cromwell against Charles I. Educated at Eton and Cambridge, he attained the highest office in his profession as President of the Chartered Land Agents Society. In religion he was a faithful Anglican: in politics a Conservative, imbued with the highest principles of a responsible and compassionate Toryism—although many in these days aver there is no such animal. Soon after I left the Estate he became a Member of Parliament, representing the local constituency, and died suddenly while contesting the seat in the 1945 General Election. (His son, Francis, is also a Member of Parliament).

The other man who was responsible for this double achievement was an Irishman, an O'Brien from County Cork, where he had been brought up very strictly as a Roman Catholic but had, when I knew him, rejected both the faith and the practices of that religion. His trade was that of an electrician in which his status was that of a foreman. He came to Llanover in the early summer of 1928 as the senior (although he was under thirty years of age) of two electricians sent down by a firm in

London to check, maintain and repair if necessary the electrical installations in the Estate Yard, Mansion, Dower House (Ty Uchaf) and the Home Farm adjoining, the power for which was generated by two large diesel engines, supported by large racks of batteries, in the Estate Yard. This was an annual event, but it was the only occasion on which O'Brien came and his coming affected me in a manner and to a degree that could not have been foreseen. He came to service the electrical system and departed having electrified me.

He was often in the office seeking information or reporting troubles and I soon sensed that this young Irishman and I might have some interests in common, so having nothing better to do in that pub-less, sleepy village after work on those evenings in early summer we arranged to meet for nothing more exciting than a walk and talk on the canal bank. I found that he was a rebel, not only against the religion in which he had been indoctrinated, but also against much else in society—not so much politically as against ideas and values by which people in those days ordered their lives. Our talk—or rather his for I was merely an appreciative listener for most of the time—was of people, mostly writers, especially poets, novelists and dramatists and he was fond of quoting passages from their works, passages which he claimed highlighted facets of the human conditions. He spoke with a slight stammer and a marked soft southern Irish accent which in my ears, attuned all day and every day to Welsh idiom and accent, seemed to add significance to all he said. To my amazement I found him to be deeply versed in Shakespeare's plays and could, and did, recite long speeches from them as well as more pithy observations. His Roman Catholicism had been replaced, it seemed to me, by a philosophy based on Fitzgerald's Rubaíyát of Omar Khayyám, as on those walks he sometimes emphasized a point in an argument by what 'our friend Omar said on the subject,' whereupon he would quote a verse or two.

Absorbed in our talk we took little note of our surroundings which presented a scene of great natural beauty: the still waters of the canal reflecting the trees, newly in leaf, that lined the opposite bank and the swans and cygnets gliding past, the fields dotted with cattle and sheep, behind them the overshadowing Blorenge mountain, with the comely Sugar Loaf and the fissured Holy Mountain rising in the far distance. We talked of the relative merits of two weekly magazines devoted largely to the topics we were discussing, 'John O'London's Weekly' and 'Cassell's.' He admired the short stories of O'Henry and encouraged me to read them which I did later and came to share his belief that some were masterpieces in that form of writing.

With nothing leading up to the question, he turned to me suddenly one evening and asked, 'What the hell are you doing here?' Taken aback, I said, 'Listening to you.' 'I don't mean that: I mean working in that Estate Office.' Had I time to reflect on the matter, I could have asked him with equal validity what he was doing working as an electrician when, with his knowledge and love of English literature, he was much better qualified to teach the subject than many who had made it their profession. As it was, I told him that I had tried to get away but in the conditions prevailing in South Wales at the time my few attempts to do so had failed, although on one occasion I had been short-listed.

Whether I described the interview that followed that short-listing I can't remember, but as what happened sheds some light on employment conditions in South Wales some sixty years ago I will do so now.

A small advertisement in the Western Mail called for a general clerk in the Earl of Plymouth's branch Estate Office at St. Fagan's Castle, near Cardiff, now the home of the Welsh Folk Museum. In addition to the ordinary skills required of a clerk in those days, book-keeping and shorthand-typing, the successful applicant would be required to serve as private secretary to the Countess when in residence and, more than that, he—in those days a 'she' was never envisaged even as a possibility —should also be able to carry out land surveying. In this last respect, I had done no more than assist the surveyor at Llanover with taking levels for water supplies and drains and had learned how to do so. I felt that with a bit of study I should be able to ascertain with some degree of accuracy the area of an irregular field or part thereof which I imagined would be all that would be called for at St. Fagan's.

I was interviewed at the head office of the Plymouth Estates in Westgate Street, Cardiff, by the agent, Colonel Forrest and his assistant. All seemed to go well until I admitted that I had never used a theodolite and, on further questioning, that I had largely forgotten the trigonometry I had been taught at school. I was then asked by the colonel what pay I expected. As I was getting fiftyfive shillings a week at Llanover I thought both the private-secretaryship and the surveying justified an extra five shillings, so mentioned £3. Consternation! 'Did I not realise,' demanded the colonel, 'that qualified surveyors, Members of the Surveyors Institution, were asking no more?' They would get in touch with me if they wanted me. They didn't. I came away feeling that perhaps at Llanover I was not so badly off after all. (Colonel Forrest was a very influential figure in those parts in those days, roads in Barry and Penarth, where the Plymouth Estates held valuable tracts of land, being named after him.)

O'Brien scoffed at my simplicity. I shouldn't wait in the marketplace with countless others for somebody to hire me: I should look round for a likely buyer and sell myself. The idea remained dormant in my mind for some weeks and then took root. I wrote to the owner of a small neighbouring estate, a leading South Wales industrialist, telling him I was under-employed (or at least not fully stretched as I liked to be), had time on my hands in the evenings and at week-ends and if I could be of any use to him I should be happy to assist. He replied at once: yes, he needed somebody like me and would I go and see him?

He was Lionel D. Whitehead of Goytre Hall, near Abergavenny, founder, chairman and managing director of the Whitehead Iron and Steel Company. On my seeing him he told me he had just been appointed a director of the large and ailing Ebbw Vale Steel and Iron Company, which, in addition to the large steelworks at Ebbw Vale, owned a large number of collieries in the area and he wished to deal with his Ebbw Vale reports and correspondence at home—away from his own company's office. He was also waging a newspaper campaign against the dumping of foreign wires to the detriment of his own company's products in that line, which again, he would prefer to do at home in the evenings. But he could not engage me thus without the approval of my employer and he would write to Lord Treowen seeking such approval. He did so, whereupon Lord Treowen becoming aware for the first time of my existence and qualifications said to Mr. Pym "If he can do that for Mr. Whitehead he can do the same for me"—or something on those lines. Thus the two birds fell to the one shot, inspired by O'Brien.

Lionel Whitehead was a man I came to respect and admire and he deserves a paragraph or two. Backward at school, so he told me (he was an Old Carthusian), he had found his niche in industry and with the founding of the Whitehead Iron and Steel Company became a pioneer in this country of the continuous re-rolling technique for reducing bars into extremely fine sheets. This, at the time of a great surge in motor car production, helped to ensure the success of his company. What also helped was his relationship with his employees. He was known to all of them and he knew many of them personally. He showed them respect and they respected him. Not content with paying them the 'going rate' he rewarded them also by a bonus based on their annual earnings at the same rate as the dividend paid to the shareholders. The bonus was often the equivalent of three weeks' pay. I knew some of the young men who 'worked on the rolls' and, possibly stimulated by some degree of envy, mentioned to Mr. Whitehead their lavish expenditure on cars (few young manual workers were able to afford a car in those days) and various entertainments. 'They must earn a lot,' I said. 'They do,' he answered, adding drily, 'And they earn it!'

Thus it came about that after finishing work in the Estate Office about 5.30, I would go to my lodgings for supper and on my bike to Goytre Hall to be there by about half-past seven for a session lasting sometimes until 10 p.m. and then cycle back in the dark and in all weathers. For two such sessions a week (sometimes a Saturday or Sunday afternoon was substituted for an evening one) I was paid £1 and thought myself lucky. With this extra money coming in I felt able to marry and did so but while on our honeymoon I read in the newspaper that Mr. Whitehead had resigned from the Board of the Ebbw Vale Company following disagreement with the chairman on measures necessary to put the company on its feet again. (He had told me that he had been shocked by the disregard shown by the management to costs. 'They have more railway engines in those works than some of the Welsh railway companies!'.)

So, soon after our marriage, his need of my services became less and in a few months I was no longer of use to him. I enjoyed the experience of working with, and for, an enlightened captain of industry. He drove himself hard and died a few years later.

Until then my work in the Estate Office had been routinely un-demanding and boring and I was required to combine my new duties as private secretary with those already held, helped by a newly appointed junior clerk. It meant a slight and indefinable rise in status and a small increase in pay. Much more imporant, it provided an insight into the mind and life-style of a man who had distinguished himself as a soldier, diplomat, Member of Parliament and, not least, in promoting and supporting as his grandmother had done, cultural interests in Wales; he was proud to regard himself as a Welshman, and a Welsh-speaking one at that.

I was amused to recall that when he had stood for re-election as a Member of Parliament in the General Election of 1911 I had done my puny best, as an eight-year-old boy, to defeat him. Living at Machen, a village just within his constituency, and believing that my parents were Conservative, I joined other boys in singing:

> Vote, vote, vote for Forestier-Walker,
> Turn old Herbert out of doors,
> Walker is the man
> And we'll have him if we can ...

After more than seventy years the last line has been forgotten but it was something like 'To-day and evermore.' (It was probably the lapel buttons given away by the Conservatives that really determined our allegiance, a practice still common in the U.S.A. but I can't remember their use in this country after 1911.)

Looking back, it seems that I, and a rapidly diminishing number of others, can claim that we worked within what was a feudal ordering of society—a system now extinct. I now see that it was a benevolent despotism, at least at Llanover under Lord Treowen, and in those harsh depression days the general feeling among us, serfs and vassals, was that we were lucky. Some, of course, myself included, were luckier than others. And if sometimes we were inclined to forget our good fortune we were occasionally brought face to face with reality by the sight, especially in summer, of small groups of unemployed miners, half-starved, pale and shabby, who had walked over the mountain, Mynydd-y-garn Fawr, from Blaenavon for a day in the country and to see how we, the other half-lived.

In these days of packaged 'convenience' foods and reliance on shops for all we eat and almost all we use, I am amazed, on looking back, by our self-sufficiency as a community. The Estate was a kingdom in miniature. In my seven Llanover years, 1927-34, a number of new houses were built to complete an attractive centre within the larger village. This was Tre Elidyr (Elidyr's town), so named after Lord Treowen's only son, killed as a soldier in Palestine in the 1914-18 War. The focal point was a wall-enclosed village green, with a memorial cross and a tablet bearing the names of all the Llanover men who had perished in that conflict. Both the long wall and the memorial were built by the Estate masons with stone taken from the Estate quarry on the mountain side above. The new houses surrounding the Green (in one of which after marriage I had the pleasure of living) were built and even tiled with the same home-produced stone by the same masons. The larch timbers forming the roofs and the oak for the doors, windows and gates had been grown on the Estate, sawn in the Estate sawmill and, in the case of the joinery, fashioned in the carpenters' shop. This dependence extended

131

Village War Memorial, Tre Elidyr, Llanover

A corner of Tre Elidyr, circa 1930

beyond life into death: after Lord Treowen became a widower in 1929, and realising that he too, then seventy-eight, might be approaching his end, he came to the Estate yard and, helped by the foreman carpenter, chose the oak planks from which his coffin would be made.

His gardens were staffed by about a dozen men and boys, controlled by the formidable Mr. Rees yr Ardd, highly knowledgeable in the arts of landscaping and horticulture, demanding of himself and his staff a devotion to duty and an integrity towards his master's time and possessions that made him feared by his underlings and respected by all. In the walled garden and greenhouses he produced fruit, vegetables and flowers in season and out of season and, apart from a fair quantity donated to charities, all for his master and his master's small family, whether resident in the country or in London, to where it was despatched in hampers by train from Nantyderry Station. The servants on board-wages, and villagers got no more than a smell of it.

We did better with the home-made cloth. The large walled-in park was dotted with his Lordship's Black Welsh Mountain Sheep, whose wool went to his water-driven mill at Gwenffrwd, tenanted and run by Jones the Weaver and his family. There, after washing, carding and spinning, it was woven into an undyed cloth, which came out a dark russet colour. From this cloth his Lordship had his country suits made. And so did I. As the pure wool was not subjected to refining by industrial processes the cloth retained much of the natural oil, which made it almost waterproof. For the same reason it had the embarrassing quality of exuding a strong odour like a wet sheep when you were caught in the rain. But it was warm and so long-lasting that suits and overcoats were discarded for shabbiness—not for reasons of wear.

He also owned two water-driven corn mills, to which the grain from the Home Farm and that of his farm tenants was sent to be ground into flour or meal for themselves and their farm animals. As well as favouring the Black Welsh Sheep (a recognized breed), the Home Farm was stocked with Welsh Black Cattle and black pigs, but I fear the last could not claim Welsh ancestry! The cows provided the milk that his two Welsh dairymaids, the sisters Lal and Annie Evans, converted into cream and butter and possibly cheese for his Lordship's table.

In season his gamekeepers produced pheasants and his riverkeepers, salmon and trout. A tree-lined stretch of the river Usk meanders cleanly through the Estate and provided excellent fishing on both banks.

The Estate had also its own 'public utilities.' The streams that flowed down from the mountains to the west had been dammed to provide mains water not only to the Mansion, farms and cottages on the Estate, but also to many properties outside its boundaries. And certain privileged homes had Estate-generated electricity. The rest of us made do with oil lamps and candles.

No commercial laundry was entrusted with his Lordship's household and personal linen. That was taken care of by laundry maids using electrically driven machines, and they dealt not only with the washing needs of the Llanover household but also with those of the house in Mayfair, to which it was returned neatly folded in large hampers, along with the fruit, vegetables, flowers, cream, butter, pheasants, salmon and so on by express train.

Where, it might be asked, did all the money come from to maintain so grand a style of living? For the new cottages in Tre Elidyr, for the new school and the village green and war memorial, as well as for the extensive programme of improvements and repairs to farm houses and farm buildings? Certainly not from the farm rents but from coal mines in the Ebbw valley where Lady Llanover had owned the Abercarn Estate and there, deep below its surface, were valuable coal seams. In spite of the deepening depression these were still being fully worked and for every ton of coal raised the colliery owners paid a levy, called a royalty, of a few pence. Many thousands of tons meant many thousands of pennies for the landowner, whose only outlay was its collection. But that fountain of wealth was soon to run dry, as within a few years of my departure the Government nationalised all mineral rights. 'And not before time!' my radical friends would have said. Agreed, but when I consider the village and farms of Llanover to-day I have to acknowledge that the money that came to Lord Treowen so easily might, in the hands of others, have been spent in ways much less commendable: it was not frittered away or squandered in what people at that time called 'riotous living.'

Lady Llanover—Gwenynen Gwent

In one respect, Lord Treowen failed his grandmother and mother, for although he spoke Welsh himself he did not insist, as they had done, that all employed at Llanover should be Welsh speaking. Had he done so my smattering of Welsh would not have been enough to qualify: I knew only enough to translate the names of common objects and those of most farms and cottages.

Thanks to Lady Llanover the village still had a Welsh chapel. She had provided the wherewithal for building and, I believe, to some extent, endowing a place of worship for those of her servants, tenants, and others who were neither Anglicans (Episcopalians) like herself, nor Congregationalist for whom there was Hanover Chapel, but Calvinistic Methodists. So far as I can recall, she attached two conditions to the benefaction. First, that the services should be in Welsh and second, that they should include the General Confession of the Anglicans, as used in their services of Morning and Evening Prayer, but of course in Welsh. That she should have required those over whom she ruled to recite this penitential prayer every Sunday, acknowledging that they had 'erred and strayed from Thy ways like lost sheep. We have followed too much the devices and desires of our own hearts. We have offended against Thy holy laws . . .' has struck me as peculiarly significant. Was it to keep them in their proper place: to ensure their continued humility and submission before her? Welsh Nonconformists, as I observed when young, showed some reluctance to acknowledge that they were sinners. Sinners were those who did not attend chapel, drunkards, adulterers and Sabbath breakers and possibly Roman Catholics. They themselves were guilty only of 'short-comings.' Lady Llanover might have seen this tendency and wished, as far as she was able, to correct it. To think otherwise, I'm sure, would be to do her an injustice.

Lady Llanover took other steps to encourage her subjects to 'live a sober life.' She converted the district into a 'dry' area. This she did by buying the two inns and turning them into temperance houses, Y Gwesty at Llanover and Seren Gobaith (The Star of Hope) at Llanelen.

Both Lady Llanover and her daughter, Mrs. Herbert, held strong political convictions and felt they had a right to impose their views on their servants and tenants: it would go hard with anyone independent or fool enough to openly oppose them. It was not uncommon in those days, especially in West Wales, for farm and cottage tenants to be evicted for open defiance of their landlord in such matters, and many victims of this form of tyranny sought and found refuge in the U.S.A.

In the General Election of 1885 Lady Llanover, in pursuance of her belief that she knew best what was good for Llanover, for Wales and for Great Britain with its then vast and powerful empire, issued a proclamation setting out 'The Right Honourable Lady Llanover's Political Opinion on the present state of Affairs.' Much as I admire the lady's achievements in other fields, time has shown that in this personal manifesto she was wrong on most counts.

Her first concern was the threatened 'Disestablishment of the Old Establish Church' (of England), a proposal she foresaw as leading 'to the destruction of all property, including every endowment now belonging to Dissenters and Nonconformists.' The Anglican church in England is still established (that is, linked politically to the State) one hundred years later, but its Welsh branch, thanks to such radical politicians as David Lloyd George, became disestablished some thirty-five years later and arose, out of the ashes, as the Church in Wales. Whether it is better and healthier for the change is for others to say, but the dire consequences feared by Lady Llanover have been avoided.

The statement proceeds: 'Her Ladyship, it is well-known, has been a good friend to both Welsh Churches and Chapels, and to those who frequent either from Religious Motives.' 'From Religious Motives!' Why on earth, one might reasonably ask one hundred years on, would anyone attend church or chapel for motives other than religious? One answer could be that in those days (and even in mine!) there was no better way on those landed estates for a tenant or employee to ingratiate himself with the owner than to be seen to be diligent in attending the church patronised by the landlord and his lady. I say church—rather than church or chapel—as I never knew of a Welsh nobleman or rich country squire ever attending a Nonconformist chapel except on special occasions like a local eisteddfod or Gymanfa Ganu—never for worship. They looked upon chapels as hotbeds of radicalism and not, as David Lloyd George demonstrated, without good reason.

Less than ten years after Lady Llanover issued her proclamation my father, then a young teenager, had an experience which throws some light on this aspect of Welsh religious life. Forsaking one Sunday his parents' Wesleyan Methodist Chapel at Machen, he went to a special service at the ancient parish church of St. Michael, to mark the completion of some works of renovation or improvement and, being shy, was glad to seat himself in the far corner of the back pew. He had not been there long, before the sound of carriage wheels heralded the arrival of persons of consequence, or so he thought, but instead some very ordinary looking men and women trooped in, filling the back row and the one in front of it. He knew none and wondered who they were. Shortly afterwards, more carriage wheels were grinding on the gravel, and this time, without doubt, personages of rank had arrived and, with great deference, were being ushered to the front row. Among them was an elderly man of some distinction, whom my father recognized as Colonel Frederick Courtenay Morgan of Ruperra Castle, Member of

Parliament, and a close kinsman of Viscount Tredegar, the principal landowner in the area, and both benefactors of the old church. The Colonel had been seated only a moment or so when he rose, turned round, and, taking an opera glass from a pocket, scanned carefully those sitting in the pews reserved for the castle servants—butler, footmen, cooks, maids, gardeners and so on. The boss was checking for defaulters! When he came to my father the scrutiny lingered so long that, in spite of his intense embarrassment, father felt disposed to put out his tongue. Obviously, the Colonel could not decide whether the lad in the corner was a new boy in the gardens, or woods, or Home Farm. The servants were of course attending 'ex officio.' That behaviour, outrageous by today's standards, would not have been so regarded by the castle servants; they would have looked upon it as allowable in one so rich and powerful, as would also the Colonel's wording of his compliment to the rector after morning service on other occasions, 'Damn good sermon, Darby!' Colonel Courtenay Morgan was a direct descendant of Sir Henry Morgan, 1635-88, the Welshman who gained fame and fortune as a buccaneer in the West Indies, and it is reasonable to suppose that with such an ancestor the Colonel felt entitled to make his own rules of behaviour.

So, while some attended because they sought to please the boss and some, like the castle servants, because they had to, there were others again, especially before the First World War, who regularly attended chapels for no better reason than to savour the sermon and enjoy the singing and stopped attending when first radio, and then television provided rival attractions. On reflection, therefore, Lady Llanover's restriction of her friendship to those who attended church or chapel 'from Religious Motives' makes sense to me: it cuts out the sycophants and the frivolous!

In considering the nature and depth of Lady Llanover's religious attitudes, I have been reminded of a story told me by my maternal grandmother some years before I went to Llanover. In the middle years of last century her mother had gone on horseback from the family farm at Bedwas over Mynydd-y-Grug to a place in the Ebbw valley, where in the open air, the renowned Baptist preacher, Charles Haddon Spurgeon, was to preach. Among the multitude attending was Lady Llanover who had come in her carriage from her other home in Gwent, Abercarn House, and had intended to sit comfortably to listen to the famous dissenter while the rest stood. But the horses and carriage took up a lot of space. So before beginning his sermon Spurgeon spoke to the lady in

137

the carriage. 'Madam,' he said, 'I have come here to preach the gospel to men and women, not to horses.' The crowd gasped at his audacity: Lady Llanover was not used to being spoken to in that way. What would she do? She got down from her carriage and stood with the rest while the coachman and footman moved off with the equipage to await her pleasure. What else my great-grandmother heard from Spurgeon on that memorable occasion might soon have been forgotten. What she could never forget was how a Baptist minister, in the words of the Magnificat, had 'put down the mighty from their seats and exalted the humble and meek.'

As for Lady Llanover, her attendance at that meeting indicates a genuine interest in religion and a willingness to accept some degree of humiliation in its observance.

This rich and learned lady also deplored 'the outcry for FREE EDUCATION' on the grounds that schooling was already 'sufficiently cheap' and that 'children's brains are overworked for useless objects . . . and are alienated from their parents.' She was opposed to young farmers being taught 'to drive the quill instead of the Plough' and to the 'daughters of workmen' learning 'the names of places in Kamchatka' instead of 'how to dress their Parents' dinners' . . . and 'how to wash and iron their own clothes.'

She ends by telling her tenants that they should suport the Government led by Lord Salisbury by voting for Mr. Rolls of the Hendre, but adds: 'Everyone here well knows that he can vote as he pleases.' 'Vote as he pleases!' The secret ballot ensured that every *man* (thirty-three years were to pass before women were allowed to vote) could vote as he pleased, but I can't imagine any Llanover tenant, still less an employee, having the audacity to espouse openly the cause of a rival candidate after her ladyship had advised otherwise.

Almost as offensive was not to vote, or at least to be reported as not voting as happened to me. In the General Election of 1931, disillusioned with politics, I could not persuade myself that any of the three candidates was worth my vote. It was a bitterly fought election, both nationally and locally, made more so in South Wales because Lord Treowen, a former Liberal Member of Parliament and until then a representative of the Liberals in the House of Lords, had gone over to the Conservatives and was exhorting other Welsh Liberals to do likewise. Nevertheless, much as I respected him and his opinions on most matters, I decided not to vote. Unfortunately for me, the sub-agent in charge of the Estate Office, my immediate superior, and, since my appointment as his Lordship's secretary, hardly a friend of mine, was acting as a teller for the Conservatives. Late in the afternoon he returned from the Polling Station to the office and told me I was free to go and vote at any time. I said I had no intention of voting. This was madness and he was clearly shaken. On realising that I had meant what he had heard, he warned me that it would be his duty to report me to the Head Agent, Mr. Pym, who in turn would feel it to be his duty to report my insubordinate behaviour to Lord Treowen. I could guess the rest: the loss of my job and, being then married, eviction for my wife and me from our very nice tied cottage. Looking back I find it hard to understand why I acted so. The sensible course would have been to have gone to the Polling Station and, if still unable to prefer one untrusted candidate to the other untrusted candidate without tossing a coin, to put in a blank paper. That night I went home confident that I would soon be jobless and homeless. Folly or bravado, or a bit of both? Or was I so dissatisfied with my job and dull existence in an 'Estate' village that I felt, come what may, I could hardly be worse off? I'm not sure; what I am sure about is that my Welsh temperament and the radical sentiments instilled in me in my youth combined to deepen a readiness to rebel at

Our 'tied cottage', 10 Tre Elidyr, Llanover

139

the slightest provocation and especially in matters where I felt, as in the right to vote or not to vote, my rights and liberties were involved.

As it was, I heard no more about it. The Conservative candidate was successful without my vote. I'm sure my offence was reported to Leslie Pym who doubtlessly thought I was a fool but not daft enough to warrant the trouble of dismissing me and the even greater one of finding and training a replacement. I'm equally sure the affair stopped with him: and that Lord Treowen was not told. I can even imagine Leslie Pym deriving some amusement from the story—these turbulent Welshmen! Certainly, he did not hold the incident against me since when he later became Conservative Member for the same seat and I was secretary to another Member, he genially entertained me at the House of Commons.

Lord Treowen

Class distinction as I saw it at Llanover was often an irritant, but it sometimes had an amusing side. In the two houses in Gwent owned and occupied in turn by Lord Treowen, Llanarth Court and Ty Uchaf, Llanover (in both of which I worked), the territory occupied by the master and his family and that inhabited by their servants were separated by a green baize-covered door. Behind it, the servants had more freedom than their master and mistress, for they could enter all rooms in which they had a duty to perform and, except for bedrooms, even without knocking (in fact to knock on the door of any ground floor room before entering was an offence calling for reprimand), but master and mistress had no such freedom in their servants' quarters. I recall an occasion when this unwritten rule was broken. Returning to Ty Uchaf for an afternoon session with Lord Treowen, I was surprised to find him standing about ten feet away from the boundary door and, for him, on the wrong side of it. He told me he had rung several times for the butler or a footman but no one had responded. I soon found the butler. He was greatly upset, not so much because he or one of his underlings had failed to respond to the bell, but by the invasion of his territory. 'Exactly how far had his Lordship stepped?' he asked anxiously. Her Ladyship, he told me, had never passed that door, which meant that Lady Treowen had, for a number of years at least, never seen her own kitchen, larders, butler's pantry, servants' hall and so on. The unwritten rule, slightly breached that day, had evolved over the centuries.

140

Llanover House, the home of Lady Llanover, demolished mid 1930s

Llanarth Court, near Raglan, Gwent, Lord Treowen's paternally descended home.
It is now a boarding school

Its great merit was that it worked and made for harmonious relations between master and mistress on the one hand, and their servants on the other. It bestowed responsibility on the shoulders of the butler and other top servants and contributed to dignity and respect between the boss and the bossed.

My duties allowed me to see what went on in both territories, sometimes when the servants were at their mid-day meal. In the housekeeper's room the butler presided at table and carved the joint or bird with dignity and skill, watched by housekeeper, cook, lady's maid and chauffeur and all waited upon by a kitchen maid. In this dining room the atmosphere was almost as baronial as in the main one: certainly the talk was more restrained and pompous. As the butler was required to address his master as 'Your Lordship' so he required the footmen to call him 'Sir'—'and don't forget it!' And they didn't forget it. (The butler had a commanding presence; tall, erect and good looking, he had been a non-commissioned officer in the Grenadier Guards during the 1914-18 War. He was Mr. Bishop and on the street could pass for one!). A very different atmosphere prevailed in the Servants' Hall. There again, in order of precedence they sat at table, housemaids, stillroom maid, kitchen maids, scullery maids, footmen and hall boy. Here talk and laughter were unrestrained and, considering their lot, their jollity was surprising. In those days no doubt they felt they were better off than their brothers and sisters.

A world of privilege! Yes, but it was also one of good order, and I noted that the privileges that Lord Treowen enjoyed were matched by acceptance in full of the responsibilities that went with them. I came to see that his whole life had been devoted to the pursuit of excellence and to what he saw to be his duty: as husband and father, as a soldier, diplomat and politician to his country, as a member of the County Council to his county, as a landowner to his tenants, as an employer to his servants and Estate employees and as the descendant of a long line of recusant Roman Catholics to God and the Roman Church.

In addition to his native English and Welsh, he spoke French, German, Italian and Russian and claimed that his knowledge of the Welsh tongue had been a great help in mastering the difficulties of Russian pronunciation. (For five years, 1886-90, he had been a Military Attaché in the Court of the Czars at St. Petersburg). His cultured voice and smooth flow of perfect English, whatever the subject, combined to make my duties as his amanuensis a never-failing pleasure.

142

I remained with him until his death in October 1933. Some friends of earlier years held that I had been working for 'an enemy of the people.' The minister of Siloam Baptist Chapel at Machen, where I had been indoctrinated in the tenets of Christianity and Socialism in the belief that they were one and the same, the gifted and eloquent Rev. Daniel Hughes, was at that time declaiming against the rich and declaring to his appreciative listeners that 'the blue blood of the British aristocrats has gone black.' Well, well! If this man I had worked for was an enemy of the people with blackish blood, then I was all for more such enemies and the blacker their blood the better. It is safe to assume that his acquaintance with the aristocracy was limited to what he had read in the newspapers and, at that time, the late twenties and early thirties, there was much lurid reporting of scandalous goings-on among the idle rich. But note that word idle!

With the passing years I have become increasingly sceptical when viewing the democratic process as demonstrated both here and in the U.S.A. It does not ensure that the cream always rises to the top. And I believe we in Britain have done well to retain both the monarchy and the House of Lords. In saying this I am following the age old pattern: the rebel at twenty becomes conventional and conforming at fifty and still more so at eighty.

I became aware that the old order of which I have written perished during the Second World War. My employer at that time, a Member of Parliament, wishing to speak on the telephone to a member of the House of Lords on a matter of some public importance asked me to 'phone the Earl's castle during the day and enquire of the butler at what time his lordship dined so as to avoid disturbing the meal. At the castle, I was answered by a man who asked for my message and assuming him to be the butler I gave it. I have not forgotten the reply. 'Please tell Sir D....... that my wife and I have a bit of supper before the library fire about eight o'clock.' It was the noble Earl himself. No butler, not dinner but supper, not the Countess or her ladyship but 'my wife.' That signalled for me the end of the old order.

I will let *The Times* have the last word. In its obituary notice it said among much else, 'By the death of Major-general Lord Treowen ... the country loses a distinguished soldier and Wales a prominent member of a family which has been associated with it for centuries. He was a particularly handsome man of distingushed appearance and in all relations of life a great gentleman.' 'A great gentleman!' What a magnificent epitaph!

143

Part V
The Davies Brothers

Margaret Davies (1818-1906) of Cwm Farm, Bedwas, Gwent, the author's great-grandmother

The Star of Wales

In my story entitled 'Caerphilly Cheese' I mentioned how, when a boy in my early teens, I listened attentively to my maternal grandmother's stories of the adventures of two of her four brothers as emigrants to the U.S.A., John Davies, born 1848 and William, born 1855.

John died in St. Paul, Minnesota in 1912, a year or so before the time of the story-telling and I had never met him. William, though living only a few miles from my home, I had seen infrequently, usually when both of us happened to be at my grandparents' farm on the same day. He was a remote figure who showed no interest in me and, until I had heard of his adventurous life in Texas, I took little note of him. That is until 1917, when I had two memorable meetings with him. On both occasions we had come to help with work on the farm. The farm was almost entirely pastoral, the only arable field being a small one used exclusively for growing root crops, but the Country War Agricultural Committee had insisted that some land should be used for corn crops.

Grandfather had complied with the order to the extent of ploughing and cultivating but having no seed drill and not knowing how to sow by hand (formerly a colliery manager, he was a reluctant farmer), Uncle William had offered to do so. It is hardly likely that he had sown corn by hand since leaving Wales almost forty years earlier but he did so that day with a skill and precision delightful to watch, as stepping out briskly and confidently, his arm moving rhythmically, he scattered the seed oats from a bag slung over his shoulder with the evenness of a machine.

He was of medium height, with a round, lined, leathery-looking face, the result of years in the Texan sun and wind. Nothing about him suggested a life of high adventure. He had a gentle manner, a soft voice and spoke slowly and hesitantly, due, I suppose, to two factors. First, he had spent many years in great open spaces in conditions of extreme loneliness, when more than a week might pass without his seeing another human being. Secondly, although he had lived many years in the U.S.A., English did not come easily to him; when speaking to my grandparents in Welsh he was much more fluent.

William S. Hart was the great cowboy hero of the cinema in those days, during and immediately after the First World War: the strong and silent stranger who rode into town, spoke only when spoken to and then in monosyllables. Physically, Uncle William did not resemble this other William in the least, but in his quietness, coolness and taciturnity he was like him and he, too, had for years carried a revolver in his belt.

147

I had little chance to talk to him when he came for the sowing but we (the man of sixtytwo and the boy of fifteen) were much together when the crop from the seed he had sown was harvested. Watching him expertly coiling a rope which had held the sheaves in place on the gambo as it made its shaky way to the rick, I asked him whether he could throw a lasso. 'No, never had need to.' 'Takes years of practice.' 'Mexican boys played with lariats from the time they could walk and they were good at it.' That opening enabled me to question him a lot about his life in the Wild West and I heard much that he had never revealed to his sister, my grandmother.

I left home shortly afterwards and did not learn anything more about Uncle William until sixty-two years later, when in 1980, revisiting Cwm Farm, Bedwas in Gwent, from which John and William had departed for America, one hundred and thirteen and one hundred and one years earlier respectively, I was told by my cousin, Jocelyn Davies, that letters the two brothers had written home were still in the farmhouse, where they had been treasured by our great-grandmother and carefully preserved by subsequent generations. Reading some of them I was fascinated not only by the experiences, pleasant and unpleasant, of the two young fortune hunters, but also by the enterprise, courage and fortitude they had shown in often daunting conditions. Here, I felt, were two stories worth telling.

Although the language of the home and chapel was exclusively Welsh, the brothers wrote home only in English, which they did imperfectly but apparently better than they could manage in Welsh, for the Welsh they spoke was not that of the Bible or their Welsh newspaper, *Seren Cymru*, but a colloquial form peculiar at that time to the area in south-east Wales in which they lived. When in his letters William essays a quotation in Welsh his spelling is often defective (but has been corrected in the extracts cited in his life story).

I expected to find in those letters tales of strange experiences in conditions of some danger in a foreign land and the stories of the lives of the two brothers are not lacking in this respect. What I did find surprising was that these adventurous young men—one facing danger from rattlesnakes and trigger-happy cowboys in western Texas and carrying a revolver for self-protection; the other, the prodigal who ran away from home with stolen money and lived and worked alongside very tough characters in the forests near the Canadian border—should ask their parents to send them a Welsh religious newspaper, *Seren Cymru*, 'The Star of Wales.' That choice of reading might be taken as no more than a measure of their homesickness but I see it as throwing light on their characters and testifying to the continuing influence on them of home and church. So a century ago 'The Star of Wales' shone in most unlikely places, including 'The Lone Star State.'

The story of John Davies—Lumberjack and Hotelier

Cwm Farmhouse, Bedwas, boyhood home of John and William Davies

My maternal grandmother told me the story of her eldest brother who had run away from home hoping to get to America but had not got out of the Bristol Channel before being shipwrecked and how, returning home crestfallen, had been welcomed by his father, not with the prodigal's fatted calf, but with a severe beating, which did not stop him making a second attempt and this time successfully. I sensed that she was an admiring and proud sister.

What I had not known and she had not felt it proper to tell me— possibly because she felt I might be tempted to do likewise—was that to ensure the success of his second escape he had stolen money from his home. Not until more than sixty years later, when in 1980 I saw the

149

letters he had written home, did I learn of this disgrace in the family history. Worse still, according to my cousin, Jocelyn Davies, the money which our great-uncle had stolen had not belonged to his parents but to Hephzibah Welsh Baptist Chapel at Bedwas, at which the family worshipped and with which our great-grandfather had a close connection, possibly as treasurer. Jocelyn had learned this from oral tradition handed down at Bedwas which had also informed him that our great-grandfather had not discovered John's second get-away until, after the boy's failure to come home for dinner, he had gone to the field he had been sent to plough and there found the team of horses standing unattended. John was nineteen.

News of where he had gone came in a letter from New York.

New York. October 22, 1867

Dear Father and Mother,

I do now write this few lines to you. I know I have done wrong but you must forgive me. I will send you the money back if you will be in want of it. Be happy and contented. I will do very well. I am now in the Yankee land. A fool is everyone who will stop there.

I will give you directions to send me a letter. I am well and happy and have had a splendid voyage.

I am yours truly,
John Davies.

John had left a home and an environment in which the common language was Welsh. He therefore thought in Welsh and the English used in his letters was a translation, which explains the strange diction used in his first letter from 'Yankee land' and his second one ('Digging coal I am now') and those that followed.

His use of the word 'there' in the last line of his first paragraph (used similarly in later letters) refers to Wales. It suggests that he was conscious of a great gap, not only in distance—an ocean apart—but also in all aspects of life. An American as soon as he stepped ashore!

Six weeks later, on December 1, 1867, he wrote from Bevier, Missouri:

Dear Father and Mother,

It is very near time for me to write to you. I am in good health and am happy. I hope you are in good health. Bevier is 1,500 miles from New York and about 70 miles from New Cambria.

Digging coal I am now. It is very good work in this country. I have worked one month and I got my pay yesterday. They pay here with banknotes. My pay was 98 dollars and 50 cents. One dollar is four shillings in your money. I do pay four dollars per week for board and washing and mending.

This place is very suitable for farmers. They can buy the land cheaper here than they pay rent for it in Wales.

Write to me as quick as you can. I will write to you after you write to me. I must conclude now with my best love to you.

John Davies

The letter is remarkable for what it doesn't say. His parents must have wondered by what means he had travelled the 1,500 miles from New York. Why, of all places, Bevier, Missouri?

A clue to this may be found in the strange equation of New York with New Cambria as points of reference, New Cambria being now so unimportant as not to appear on any of the several maps I have looked at, yet John assumes the name would be known to his parents. This fact and the name itself, Cambria being a Latinised form of Cymru (Wales), indicate that it was a Welsh settlement to which he had been directed.

Almost all John's letters begin by saying he is well and expressing the hope that his parents also are well and generally these sentiments will be omitted from following extracts, as will also his various subscriptions, ranging from 'Yours faithfully' to 'Your affectionate son.'

He lived very much in the present—natural in a nineteen-year-old— and seldom feels obliged to mention why he left his last job or any intention of changing to another. The past is behind, the future unknown, sufficient for the day was to feel and to say he was well.

Another feature of his letters is their constant reference to the prices of farm land, the state of the farm crops and the prices realized for them. Wherever he goes he is appraising land values and crop yields and prices. Although young, his farming background impels his gaze to the good earth and the benign or cruel sky and he feels that this is a subject of prime importance and worthy of report to his father and brothers, who are farming in less favourable conditions on the lower slopes of a Welsh mountain.

A gap of eleven months and then the twenty-year-old boy writes:

Nov. 7, 1868. Rushville, Shuyler County, Illinois

I am now in Illinois driving a waggon for the railroad company. They are building a new railroad. I am hauling provisions for the men to live on. I have a two-day journey to go every time and very often I am driving all day and all night.

I would send the money back if I could get some British money. This paper money is no good there.

So, in just over a year, John has saved enough money to repay his unsanctioned loan. Three months later he is still working for a railroad company but one already operating:

I did not go down to Kansas as I expected but am a brakesman on the Chicago, Burlington and Quincy railroad, Lewistown branch. The train I am on runs from Galesburg to Rushville, a distance of 200 miles, a passenger train. There is not as much danger on the trains there (Wales) as on these here.

Braking is a good job, very good wages, 75 dollars a month. The way I got in is I met the conductor of the train as I was going to start for Kansas, a Welshman. He discharged the brakesman and took me on. I count myself lucky.

On May 29, 1869, while still at Lewistown he writes again and after reporting on the fine spring and the promise of 'a very large crop of wheat,' continues:

I suppose you have heard of the connection of the Pacific Railroad in Utah Territory. I will send a newspaper with a picture of the connection in it. I have a good deal of money saved now.

I am on the lightning express train running from Chicago to Quincy, a distance of 268 miles, carries the mail, stops only once in that distance, runs at 50 miles per hour, a safer place than I was before as our train runs at such a rate they take more care about it.

If the poor men of Wales was over here now, how much better they would be. A man would not have to wait five minutes for work even in the towns . . . could not walk the streets without being accosted by someone wanting hands.

Six weeks later, writing from Rockford, Illinois, he says he was working on a passenger train running from Chicago to Rockford and assures his parents, who had obviously worried about his safety, at a time when derailments and other accidents were featured frequently in their newspapers, that they need not fear he would get hurt, as 'there is not so much danger here as there is on the railroads there.' He had apparently forgotten his earlier statement to the contrary.

Nevertheless, John goes on to inform them that if perchance he was injured 'the company would write to you and tell you all about it.' I can't imagine anything he could say that would be less reassuring.

The good harvest he had foreseen in the spring had already begun and he was amazed to discover that farm hands were being paid five dollars a day 'or in your money one pound.'

The next letter to survive is dated March 10, 1870 and comes from Helena, Arkansas, which he had probably reached by river steamer as it stands on the west bank of the Mississippi. He describes it as 'quite a large town,' even 'larger than Caerphilly' which then had a population of fewer than 3,000. He does not say how he came to be there or what he was doing, but remarks:

A very heavy tornado passed over this place about two weeks ago, several persons got killed, some frame houses were lifted in the air and some steamers were wrecked.

Two months later, May, 1870, John believes he has found an earthly paradise, another Garden of Eden, blessed with luscious fruits: the place is Eunice, Chicot County, Arkansas.

He is only 21 and has become a plantation manager for a Mr. Oscar Bowles whom he describes as a Virginian and a Justice of the Peace.

On this occasion he says how he came to change his job and find another further south: 'I left the business I was at because Mr. Bowles persuaded me and offered better wages.' Later he says that he boards at Mr. Bowles' house and is 'treated just like his own child.'

The three letters he wrote from Eunice, all in the summer of 1870, are long, rambling and a bit repetitive, but the following extracts show that he marvelled at the fertility of the region, was fascinated by its wild-life and proud of his standing as a manager to be trusted with the care of the business in the owner's absence.

> You have no idea of the variety of fruits, of the most delicious kinds, pineapples abundant, bananas, oranges and lemons. Farmers here can keep all the cows they want without feeding them in the winter. The soil is very rich and you can raise 60 to 75 bushels of oats to the acre and 50 bushels of barley.
>
> The land is too rich to grow wheat, but the most profitable crop is cotton. An average of 20 pounds worth of cotton to the acre. One person can plant and pick 10 or 12 acres of cotton a year.
>
> They raise about 60 bushels of maize or Indian corn per acre; sells for about $1 per bushel. This plantation this year had about 400 acres of cotton.
>
> I live on the banks of the Mississippi River, about a mile and a half wide here. Spring rains and snow thawing up north has swollen the river so that it is overflowing the banks at present (May, 1870).
>
> The planters have to do everything in canoes. Whenever they want to go to the shop or anything, they have to get in a boat. The high water does not affect this plantation as it is back from the bank.
>
> The steamers are continually running. They will land if you will make motions to them. By sending an order for anything you want, they will fetch it and you pay on delivery.

A swamp lay between the plantation and the river which, with the wildlife, he described thus:

> A swamp, thick with the growth of cypress trees, some 50 yards high, and on the ridges cane bush grows, so thick that a man cannot walk through it. In this cane there is plenty of deer, and I have shot seven.
>
> Plenty of bear and panther here, too, wild cat, raccoon and possum; also all kinds of game, small and large, and in the rivers and bays plenty of fish; in the

153

lakes plenty of alligators, same as the African crocodiles; some monkeys in the forest of a small species.

On other matters, both local and international:

Two new railroads building now from this place, one running in a north direction and the other direct west. They will carry everything in and out from the Mississippi River which will make a large town of this place even.

The country is getting settled quick. Hundreds of men around the neighbourhood working on the railroads, nearly all Irish. (And with a touch of nostalgia, he adds, 'I would like to know if there has been much building going on in Bedwas since I left.')

Everywhere there is a great deal of talk about the war and everybody thinks that England will get into it. I would be very much obliged to you if you would send me the London Times or bundles of miscellaneous newspapers.

(Presumably he is referring to the Franco-Prussian war). There is much in these and later letters to suggest that his parents were anxious about him and pressing him to return home—the prodigal had been forgiven. His excuse at Eunice was that Mr. Bowles was going away that summer, leaving John, in spite of his youth and inexperience, in charge of the plantation.

Everything indicates that he was a sober, hard-working and responsible young man. That he was also a little homesick is also shown in two brief requests: 'Please send me the Seren Cymru (a Welsh language newspaper). I would like to see it very much.' And in a postscript, 'Please remember me to my old friends.'

The next surviving letter was written fifteen months later, Jan. 22, 1872, from St. Paul, Minnesota. That he had written home at least once in the meantime, apparently from Hudson, Wisconsin, is obvious as is also that, as usual with him, he had not considered it necessary to explain why he had forsaken Chicot County, Arkansas, which in one of his letters from Eunice he had confidently described as 'one of the finest places in the world.'

Dear Father and Mother,

Hoping that you are all well and doing well. I received your last letter in Hudson and was very glad to hear from you. I have been working in the pineses, or you may understand better, the pine forest.

About two weeks ago I received a very serious accident, a very bad cut in my foot with an axe and I had to come to St. Paul to get it doctored. Dr. Smith has been attending to it.

You asked in your last letter what was the reason I left the south. It was not healthy enough in summer time for me to live there. I had the ague or inter-

154

mittent chills and fever and I am not rid of them yet. The summer I stayed there I came near to dying of typhus fever.

The south is good enough in winter but in summer when the hot sun pours down on the swamps and marshes of the Mississippi bottoms, it is too sickly for a man that is not acclimatised to live there.

It was a long way to come up here, but this is very healthy country but very cold in winter. Snow on the ground from the first of December till the middle of March, very few Welsh in this place, a very large immigration, mostly from Sweden and Norway. St. Paul is a large town, about 30,000 inhabitants.

The smallpox is in this part of the country at present. I am staying at a boarding house. Boarding and lodging cost me $5 a week. When I cut my foot, I was 70 miles from here.

Four months later he was back in the 'pineses' and, writing from Carver, Minnesota in May, 1872, he says more about the injury he had suffered.

It was a very bad foot, cut clean through about two inches above the toes. All the bones except the bone of the big toe was cut clean through. The doctor thought he would have to cut the foot off but it healed all right. He charge me $50.

That charge must have rankled long in his mind. Later in the same letter he reports that times were 'very good, work plentiful and good wages,' with farm hands getting from $25 to $30 a month, so his doctor's bill equalled roughly two months' wages of a farm hand.

In the same letter, he describes another alarming experience:

I was in the pineses in Wisconsin the time of the great fire, cutting timber for the sawmill. We knew the fire was coming two days before it came. We could see clouds of smoke in the sky. It came like a volcano.

We had a temporary house built of squared timber. We kept it wet with water, and around the house for 200 yards we burnt clear of everything.

When the fire came around us, the heat was tremendous. The fire travelled about seven miles an hour; it appeared to come in one solid mass and reached from the ground to the top of the trees. It burnt over hundreds of miles. About four miles from us, four Norwegians got burned to death.

Neither the accident to his foot nor the forest fire, which together would have induced most men to seek another way of earning a living, stopped him from returning to the 'pineses' of Wisconsin and Minnesota where the environment and the challenge of hard and dangerous work obviously appealed to his adventurous nature and the relatively high rate of pay to his ambition to become at least moderately rich.

Possibly in response to appeals from his parents to return home in almost every letter, he makes a promise to do so, but in the future—the present was not convenient.

He could not have been afraid of his father's wrath, for the money stolen had been repaid and added to, and plainly he had been forgiven. The answer must be that having had a taste of travel and adventure, he was afraid of becoming trapped for life in 'the trivial round and common task' of a farm set in a beautiful but sleepy fold of the Welsh hills. So began eleven years of hard and dangerous toil as a lumberman, during which, in 1876, his father died.

After spending the winter of 1872-3 in Duluth, where he 'did not do much work . . . times very dull,' he wrote from Ashland on April 29th 1873 saying that he had been working all that spring 'log driving' on a river between Ashland and Duluth and that he had been paid high wages because of the very dangerous nature of the work, which he described as rolling the logs into the river, mounting them to push them into the stream and thus running them down river into a bay on Lake Superior. There was naught for his parents' comfort as he explains what happens when a man falls off between or under the crashing logs, an ever present risk in spite of the spiked soles of their boots. He adds that he was wet all the time, a condition which must have caused him extreme discomfort and it is a testimony to his robust health that he does not mention any ill effects. However, whether because of the hardships and dangers of his work as a lumberman, he expresses an intention to return to the work he had in the previous autumn, which only now we learn was as an axeman with the surveyors of the Wisconsin Central Railroad.

Still at Ashland, when he wrote in the following October, he reported that the summer had been marked by many heavy storms with 'a great many steamers and sailing vessels lost' on Lake Superior and that, in spite of 'dull times', he had been busy. The 'dull times' referred to the demand for labour but they had been dull for him socially also. He was uncertain whether to remain at Ashland 'all winter or not' and adds there is 'only one other Welshman here and he is from North Wales.' That meant that each would regard the other as speaking Welsh like a foreigner! The letter proceeds, 'He takes one Welsh paper Y Drych every week, a Welsh paper printed in Utica, State of New York. I will send one of them to you.'

He remained at Ashland for the winter and, on March 15th 1874, reported that he was earning 'very good wages, running a circular saw (60 inches in diameter) in the Ashland Sawmill, a large steam mill.' He went on to describe Ashland: '. . . a new town. Three years ago there was only four houses here but now there are five thousand inhabitants, four churches, two school-houses and a large library.' The fact that he mentions churches, schools and a library but not hotels, inns and saloons may indicate what institutions were of interest to him, and his sober habits may also be deduced from his concluding sentences: 'I cannot tell when I will come home. I have plenty of money to come if I want to.'

Whether in response to requests or of his own volition, he had from time to time gone to some trouble to send home 'likenesses.' In a letter from Ashland in January, 1874, he promised to send a photograph when he could get one taken, but explained there was 'no place this side of Duluth and that is 100 miles away.'

A year later he makes good his promise and a ferrotype of him that has survived may be one taken in Duluth when he was twentyseven. It shows a young man with a round, unlined, innocent, almost handsome countenance, deeply serious, carefully dressed, and looking every inch a gentleman—a lawyer, doctor or minister, perhaps—and bearing no resemblance to the tough lumberman of his letters. That 'likeness' must have given his mother some comfort.

Tintype photo of John believed to have been taken in 1875 when he was 27

157

On August 18th 1874, writing from Clear Lake, Polk County, Wisconsin, he had little to report, but he was 'getting along first rate.' On January 24th 1875, while still at that address, he apologised for his failure to write because he had 'been up in the lumber forest for a long time' as 'foreman for Knapp Stout & Co.' and that he was going 'right back again into the woods.'

More than a year later, by which time his parents must have given up hope of his continued existence, he wrote, on February 6th 1876, from New Richmond, Wisconsin. After apologising for failure to write more often he explains that he had been too busy, having been over three months in the pine woods as foreman over a gang of 28 cutting timber, not, he adds, 'an easy position.' They had 36 horses (six to a sleigh) and six oxen for pulling the logs together for loading. After another month they would begin to run the timber down river.

The following winter he is back in the woods, this time at Clayton, Polk County, Wisconsin. Although he was 'getting along very well' there were more men out of employment than he had ever seen at home and he blamed the presidential election which 'had caused so much trouble . . . that everything is unsettled.'

Again, almost a whole year went by before his next letter. On November 19th 1877 he wrote from Pine City, Pine County, Minn. This time his failure to write earlier was because he had 'been up river putting in a dam,' and when the job had been finished instead of allowing him 'to come down' the company had sent him up Snake River to build a house and stables where he was to remain for the winter.

After his father's death in 1876, John's letters became less frequent. The next to survive—and there may have been few in between—is dated April 14, 1881.

In the meantime he had been joined temporarily by his younger brother, William, who after landing in New York in 1879, wrote to his mother: 'John and the boys are well.' (The 'boys' must have been fellow Welshmen known to both John and William and employed by John.)

In his next letter, clearly in response to his mother's questions, William reports on John thus:

> 'John is not changed much since he came from home . . . not very fluent in the Welsh language now, he much rathers to speak English. He has got the same twang as the American exactly when speaking.'

If John's Welsh had become rusty, his letters show a continual improvement in his use of English.

He gave William employment for a time but William had no liking for work in the woods, nor the cold of the North, and soon departed to make a life for himself as a farmer in Texas.

John's letter of April 14, 1881, written at Hudson, Wisconsin, begins.

Dear Mother,

I think I ought to write you a few lines to let you know how I am doing. I have been so busy since I wrote to you last that I have had no time to write. I have a large amount of men working for me all the time. Sometimes 100 and sometimes 300. I am making money very fast.

The wording suggests that he had now become a contractor in his own right in the lumber business.

The letter proceeds as if what follows was of secondary importance and interest to his mother:

I got married about one month ago to Miss Emma Kingsley of Medford, an American girl. I will send you a photo of both of us . . . I have been very lucky these few last years and have made a pile of money and my prospects at present are very encouraging.

Presumably eleven months passed before John wrote again. In the meantime he had moved his home, if not his business, into eastern Minnesota, and from Stillwater in that state on March 14, 1882, he wrote:

It is a very long time since I wrote to you . . . I am almost ashamed to write. Me and wife are well at present and doing well. Lewis Williams and George are about 70 or 80 miles away from where I am. They got a job on another railroad.

I have got a very comfortable home in Stillwater, a town of about 10,000 inhabitants on the river St. Creux. I am not all the time at home as my business calls me away . . . I think there is few happier couples living than myself and little wife.

It is not as lonesome as it was for me. I was for years among strangers that did not care for no one. My wife sends her best love to you. Remember me to Elizabeth and the boys. So no more at present from your loving and undutiful son.

'Loving and undutiful son!' I find that subscription, used only in this letter, both significant and heart-warming. Had marriage and home making caused him to reflect on the degree of heartache which his flight from home and his continuing failure to go back even for a short visit might have entailed, especially in his mother?

Stillwater March
14th 1882

Dear Mother
It is so long since
I wrote to you before I am allmost
~~ashamed to~~ write to you me
and wife are well at present
and doing well and i hope you
are the same i have not a
had a letter frome William
for a long time not since i
herd frome home last
i would like to hear frome
him but i do not know
his address or i would write
to him i am living about
six miles from the place
where i was when i wrote
to you last

Lewis Williams and George
are about 70 or 80 miles
frome me they get a job
on another Railroad
i have been very busy all
winter - and expect to be
all summer i have got a
very comfortable home
in stillwater, stillwater
is a town of about
10000 inhabitants on the
river St Croix on the line
between Wisconsin and
minnesota i am not all
the time at home as my
business calls me away pert
of the time but i think
that there is a few happier
couples living than myself
and little wife

it is not as lonesome
as it was for me .
s was for years among
strangers that did not care
for no one but themselves
but is different with me
now — my wife sends
her best love to you
remember me to Elizebeth
and the boyes
so no more at present
from your Loving an
undutifull son
J T Davies
Stillwater
Minn.
U.S.

Facsimile of John's letter of March 14th 1882 in which he subscribes himself 'Your loving and undutiful son'

In September 1882, again from Stillwater, he reported that the summer had been the best he had ever seen. But he was thinking naturally, only of the farmers whose crops had been 'unusually good,' since he goes on to mention 'a terrible lot of sickness, diphtheria and typhoid fever . . . and men and women carried away by the hundreds.'

This was quickly followed in November by a letter mostly given over to comments on the weather and the farm crops; he is impressed by the fact that wheat was yielding generally 20 to 30 bushels per acre, 'sometimes as high as 40 bushels,' but even more by a new invention, a machine that cut and bound it 'with cord at the same time.'

The next letter to survive was written in March, 1887, and it is from his wife. They had moved to St. Paul, a town, she says of 50,000 inhabitants. She acknowledges her husband's failure to write as often as he should and promises to make up for his neglect, but offers no excuses.

She says they had 'not been blessed with children' and were 'getting along very well' . . . 'business is good' . . . 'and we do not want for anything of this world's goods.'

His wife wrote again from St. Paul on Oct. 30, just five months later, and asks to be informed of John's age: he had 'got a little mixed up as he has been away from home so long,' but thought he was 36 or 37. (He was 39). She gives her own age as 26, which means she was married at 20.

A further five months and in April 1888, came the last but one of their retained letters, reporting that times in Minnesota were 'real good' and enclosing a present, a draft for twenty pounds, and again apologising for their inability to go 'home' as to do so would involve neglect of their business. What their business was is not even hinted at.

The last of the letters was written five years later, December, 1893, and their business at that time is revealed in the printed address:

TRANSIT HOUSE,
J. T. Davies, Proprietor,
New Brighton, Minn.

So he had become an hotel keeper, a fact which must have surprised his family greatly, for their roots were in the land. It is written by his wife and part is missing. She says 'John is in very good health, weighs 230 pounds.'

At that time, when tuberculosis was so rife, excessive weight was looked upon with favour: we know better now, and this fact might have had some bearing on the circumstances related in the epilogue.

Epilogue

In the summer of 1912, his youngest brother, William, who had followed John to the United States and, after making a small fortune as a sheep farmer in Texas had then returned to Wales, received a letter from the cousin, George Williams, mentioned in the letter of March 14, 1882:

Transit House
New Brighton, Minn.
J. T. Davies, Proprietor
Rates $1.50 per day

June 5, 1912

Dear Cousin William,

It is my painful duty to inform you of your brother Jack's death which occurred Wednesday a.m. June 5th at St. Joseph's Hospital, St. Paul, Minn., caused by Bright's disease from which he has suffered more or less for some time. He was in the hospital two days only . . . He made a will which is now in Probate Court . . . It was his wish that I act as his Executor . . .

The executor had entered on his duties with commendable promptitude and instead of finding that the deceased 'was pretty well fixed' as he had expected, he had discovered a condition of near bankruptcy. He explains why in the following terms:

'When the packing house and stockyards were in operation and Mrs. Davies alive, they made and saved lots of money. The packing house burned down in 1893 (never rebuilt), the stock yards moved away in 1893, Mrs. Davies died in 1894.

Since then he has been going back and running the place at a daily loss with hired help who helped themselves and friends to all drinkables, eatables and smokeables they possibly could without detection.

Also the waste in the kitchen was fearful. Jack seldom went in there—just took the helps' word for everything . . . His business neighbours and myself who had seen how things were carried on told him of it. All the satisfaction we got was he knew what he was doing and needed no advice.'

The executor and his wife had at once stepped into the hotel and taken over the management in an attempt to salvage what they could of the business before disposing of the property, but he could offer little hope that the four beneficiaries under the will—the sister and two brothers in Wales and himself—could expect much after all the debts were paid, including one 'of about $2,000 to Haines Brewery for beer alone.'

It is a painful tale of mismanagement: over-stocking of perishable foods, e.g. '400 dozen eggs packed in the cellar, now more than half spoiled,' and lack of supervision over untrustworthy and reputedly dishonest servants (he had a staff of five when he died). In such conditions, the business would have failed eventually in any case, Hotel keeping was certainly not his line and it is probable that he was lured into it by his wife, who, without children, and liking that way of life had made a success of it until her untimely death at the age of 33.

So John Thomas Davies, born at Bedwas, Gwent in 1848 and died at St. Paul, Minnesota in 1912, leaving no issue and little in worldly goods, had at least 'made good' in the land of his adoption.

Until his wife's death he could look back upon twenty seven years of adventure and achievement, which almost certainly would have eluded him if, as a dutiful son, he had remained on his father's farm in the mountains of his native Wales.

The story of William Davies—Texan shepherd

Unlike his eldest brother, John, who had run away from home in circumstances that, in the language of those days, 'brought shame on the family,' William left home with his family's blessing. He might have felt that with two younger brothers there was no scope for three of them on the farm and by that time John was writing home telling them of wonderful opportunities in America. He left this country in July 1879, when he was twenty-four years of age, and reported his arrival in New York in a letter to his mother, his father having died three years earlier.

New York
Aug. 7, 1879

Dear Mother,

I have arrived safe in good health after fourteen days voyage having had splendid weather, but I was very sick for five or six days. We were about fifty passengers on board. She had a cargo of tin and twenty cows and a bull of the Alderney breed and I was very lucky to have a drop of milk now and then. They were very kind on board. We had plenty of food and amusement. So we are off again for Wisconsin. I will write after I get there. So goodbye for the present from your loving son,

William Davies

New York
Aug 7th 1879

Dear Mother
            I have arrived
safe in good health after,
fourteen days voiage having
a splended weather but I
was very sick for five or
six days we where we where
about 50 passenger on board
she had a cargo of tin and
20 cows and bull Alderney
breed and I was very

lucky to have a drop of
milk now and then
they where very kind on board
we had plenty of food and
amusement. So we are
off again for Wisconsin I
will write after I get
there so goodbye for
the present. From your
loving son
William Davies

Facsimile of William's letter of Aug. 7th 1879 announcing his arrival in New York

'So we are off again to Wisconsin' suggests that, as was often the case, he was with a party of young men from the Bedwas area. Wisconsin was their destination because John was in Wisconsin and in a position to offer them employment in the pine forests.

In a short letter dated Sept. 28th he reports his arrival at Cumberland, Barron County, Wisconsin, but as a true farmer his thoughts turn naturally to the harvest at home for which, he hopes, they have had good weather, and missing the fields and open landscape of his Welsh home, he tells his mother that at Cumberland 'there is no clear land within twenty miles, here it is all timber'. The letter ends with an urgent request for the address of a Joseph Nicholas 'that's living down in Kansas.'

In his next letter, again from Cumberland and dated Oct. 26th, he is obviously answering questions for, as with me, his mother wished to know more about the voyage and the journey from New York to Wisconsin. He writes:

> ... About the voyage, we had splendid weather on the sea, but I was never so sick in my life as I was the first week ... there was three Welshmen from the Rhondda valley and two Englishmen from Cwmbran coming with us ... About a dozen of us went to stay at the Bristol Arms where we had good lodgings.
>
> New York is very large and there is great traffic there. There are railroads going all through the town above the streets ... fixed on iron pillars ... then we booked ourselves to Milwaukee, Wisconsin. But as the train was due in Milwaukee at twelve o'clock at night we came out in Chicago at six o'clock on Saturday night.
>
> When we rose on Sunday morning we were very surprised to see the streets full of carriages and wagons and all the stores open as the day before. We started again on Sunday morning for Cumberland. We was fourteen days coming from New York, cost very near twenty pounds altogether ...

At Cumberland the party of friends was met by William's cousin, Lewis Williams, and the letter proceeds:

> 'Lewis was on the platform when we arrived and he stared very much at us. He couldn't quite believe himself that we were there. John (Williams's brother) was up in the woods about thirteen miles and Tom was eight miles below Cumberland. John came down next day when he heard that we were there. He is not changed much since he came from home.
>
> I would know him very well. He is not very fluent in the Welsh language now, he much rathers to speak English. He has got the same twang as the American exactly when speaking. I went up with him in a few days to work. I do have good wages with him, about six pounds and board a month—more than I would have with anyone else.

He was very glad to receive the present from you and Eliza (his sister). He is doing very well . . . got a good deal of money in St. Paul's Bank, but I don't know how much . . . He is doing about two pounds a day very often now with this contract. Wages is about a dollar and a half a day here and we pay three and half dollars for board. Beef is five cents a pound.

All the part around here is flat . . . nothing but timber and lakes for twenty miles around here. I don't like to be in this part very well . . . I have been here for two weeks . . . to St. Paul's Fair, Minnesota, and I travelled a lot in that state . . . I came back to Stillwater . . . to cut Indian corn for a Welsh farmer there at a dollar a day and board. He is a man from Llaniltid, S.W. (South Wales) . . . My journey cost ten dollars and I made ten dollars by cutting corn, £2 . . . I don't think I will be in this place very long . . .'

So after just nine weeks he had decided that the pine forests of northern Wisconsin had no attraction for him notwithstanding the high wages earned by the lumbermen and the companionship there of his brother and other Welshmen: he was determined 'to go it alone' in the great open spaces of the plains.

Indeed, as he wrote the letter he must have been contemplating an immediate departure, spurred on, no doubt, by the onset of the northern winter, as only fourteen days later he wrote from Fort Worth, Texas, having, by his own reckoning, travelled 2,500 miles, and made an unplanned, but hoped for, diversion in Kansas, where he called on the Joseph Nicholas whose address he had requested in his letter of Sept. 28th.

Forth Worth, Texas
Nov. 9, 1879.

Dear Mother,

I take the pleasure to write to you a few lines . . . I arrived here about four days ago after travelling about 2,500 miles from Wisconsin. I did not remember the address Joseph gave me about his uncle but one day I remembered the word Emporia. So I went there and they told me he was about twelve miles from town. I went there and they were very kind to me. They were doing well . . . Eighty head of cattle and eighty acres of land but they don't keep their cattle on the prairie outside their land. It was very cold there and they have to bring their cattle to the yard at night to feed them . . . I saw it was to cold there and came down here to Texas.

I was a few days here looking for work as it is very dull here in the fall but I got work with a farmer living six miles from the town. He has over three hundred head of cattle and I like the place very well. Here a man can make money fast by keeping sheep or cattle as he can keep them for nothing as there is plenty of grass here in winter as well as in summer.

People do become rich here in a short time if they have the means to start. I am thinking to stay here till the middle of February, then I will buy a pony to go a few

hundred miles west to the sheep and cattle ranges; it is very dear to go by coach
. . . a man can tie his blanket and food on the pony . . . there is plenty of work to
herd sheep in the west in the springtime.

From your affectionate son,
William Davies.

Four months later, on March 7th, 1880, he reports having found
work with 'a big contractor,' who had 'taken five miles of the Texas
Pacific (railroad) to work . . . eighty miles out west (from Forth Worth),
with ten teams and wagons.' There were about ten men to a team,
including a cook and it would take them about four days to reach the
site.

His mother had asked what he was doing on Sundays, an enquiry
prompted, no doubt, by William's account of Sunday morning in
Chicago where he had been amazed to see shops open and street traffic
just as on an ordinary weekday. In those days, as also in my early days,
Sunday was a day of quiet and peace in the Rhymney Valley. On that
day no trains ran on the Brecon and Merthyr Railway and the road
traffic was confined to horse drawn vehicles taking families to and from
the churches and chapels in the valley. At Cwm Farm attendance at the
Welsh Baptist Chapel at least twice on the Sabbath was mandatory for
both parents and children. To make this possible, and in obedience to
the fourth commandment—to keep holy the sabbath day—no manner of
work was done that could be put off till Monday. Brought up in this
tradition and remaining a dutiful son, William was both honest and
daring in his answer: 'washing, mending, reading, writing, shooting
and riding,' as while his mother might recognize the need for the first
four activities it is hardly likely she would find it easy to accept the last
two pleasures as unavoidable.

He goes on to say that he was living in a boardinghouse kept by an
English couple from Sheffield, that he had arrived in Texas four months
earlier with only ten shillings ($2.50), but 'without spending one cent' he
had saved eight pounds ($40).

But the money had not come easily as to earn it he had had to work
'twice as hard as at home' and he felt that working for other people was
'bondage' to him. He discourages others at home from following him
unless they come as a group, 'colony.'

The letter ends with a statement which gives credence to other stories,
and films based on them, concerning life on the frontier in those days:
'A man must be persevering and courageous here as there is twice the
temptation here as there (Wales) and to have a friend here is impossible.'

170

William was no fool and in deciding to remain in Texas he knew what he was letting himself in for. And in a postcript: 'Excuse my bad writing as I have no time and in the middle of other people.'

Two months later, writing from San Angelo, two hundred miles west of Forth Worth, he reported that he had become a shepherd, but not until five months and several letters later does he report an accident suffered whilst still at Forth Worth and then only in response to a question from home regarding his health.

He had cut his foot with an axe and explains how it happened:

> Another man and me had gone to the woods for two waggon loads of wood. I was a little careless while cutting the limbs from a tree, the axe glanced and cut a big gash in the foot, just in the butt of my toes, cut only one tendon. We could not stop it bleeding for a while till my partner filled the cut with 'bacco.
>
> Then the boss came and I had this horse and rode seven miles to town and the doctor put three tacks in it, cost two dollars. Then I could not put my foot to the ground for two weeks, but my partner made a pair of crutches for me.
>
> As nobody could milk but myself, so I hopped along to milk four cows night and morning. In the daytime I had one hundred sacks to patch . . . and I chucked corn (pulled the leaves off the Indian corn) as I did not lose a single day.

The letter of May 24th, 1880 calls for quotation almost in full as in it he describes the life of a Texan shepherd with a succinctness that defies abbreviation.

Why he had left the railroad construction gang so soon after joining is never explained.

Fort Concho
May 24, 1880

> I am now a shepherd herding sheep to the man I was shearing for . . . We had seven thousand sheep to shear as other men's flocks came here to be shorn. Mr. Arding here has three thousand two hundred sheep without the lambs and they average six and a half pounds per head of wool. The flock I am herding is two miles from the ranch, by the side of the river, and I've got one thousand seven hundred sheep in the flock. My wages are one pound ($5) a week and my board . . .
>
> My day's work . . . rise at half past four, cook my breakfast and milk my three goats. Start out with my flock at five o'clock—sunrise—and back again at eleven to the water. They will then go to the shade under the trees for about four hours.
>
> In that time I will be baking and cooking and doing everything I want to . . . Start out again and at dusk . . . have my supper, then I will roll up in my blanket on the ground by their side.
>
> My provisions are bacon, flour, rice, dried apples, beans and plenty of milk. I make my bread with sour dough (seir dasu y Phariseaid) you know. (Seir dasu y Pharisaid—leaven of the Pharisees).

I don't see a man for days sometimes . . . no Sunday here: it is the same every day.

Mr. Arding's wool will amount this spring to over one thousand pounds and the increase in his flock this year will amount to very near two thousand pounds. He came here from California four years ago next fall with one thousand four hundred sheep and he was two hundred pounds in debt to his shepherd. Now he has a fine house . . . He intends to stop here a few years then sell out and go east. And he is no exception. They are all doing just as well . . . No disease here among sheep, no worm or maggots.

William's ambition is fired by these facts and figures. At twenty five he is healthy, strong and confident and obviously unusually self-reliant. He goes on to ask his mother to send him at once a Banker's Draft for three hundred pounds ($1,500), in accordance with a promise made to him before leaving, as he planned to buy sheep in October.

He renews the request in a letter four weeks later and asks for the draft to be sent to San Antonio 'about two hundred miles from here' where he intends to make his purchases and calculates that it would take him about two months to bring them to the Fort Concho area where he thought the land was suitable and cheap. But, as he explains, he couldn't spend all the loan on sheep: he needed also 'a light waggon, two ponies and cooking utensils.'

San Antonio, Texas
August 26, 1880

Dear Mother,

I received your letter dated 2nd August yesterday and was very glad to hear from you . . . I had just arrived from a trip out west where I had been looking for sheep . . . over two weeks and I travelled about two hundred and fifty miles on my pony. There are no fences and plenty of grass all over. I lived on bread and bacon and molasses which I cook myself.

Sheep are much dearer now than they were six months ago, but I think I can get them cheaper here in San Antonio than out in the country.

. . . This piece of poetry that you sent me is very affecting, so I must conclude with best love.

From your affectionate son,

William Davies.
Box No. 240
San Antonio, Texas

P.S. I will expect the money in about twelve days. Please excuse my bad writing as I write this out on the prairie on the saddle.'

It is interesting to note, one hundred years later, that his mother's letter from Wales to San Antonio, Texas had taken just twenty three

172

days. Today, by surface mail, I don't think this time would be bettered by a single day.

On 1st October, writing from Culebra Springs, Helotes Post Office, Bexar County, he acknowledges the draft from home which he says brought in $960 exchanged at $4.80 which meant that his mother had sent £200 instead of the £300 asked for. He doesn't complain. He bought three hundred and fifty ewes at two and a half dollars which accounted for $875.

> I think this is the best bargain I have seen but I could have bought sheep at $1 a head but they were Mexican sheep and would bring lambs all through the winter and most would die . . . But these (the ones he had bought) I know what they are . . . I have been herding them for three weeks before I bought them. I settled with him to put his rams with them, for he has got good rams—thoroughbred Merinos—and they shear over twenty pounds of wool per head . . . I think my flock will average three pounds of wool per head.
>
> I do herd six hundred head of lambs for this man with my flock and he pays me $12 per month for herding and board and grass . . . I will make a little money by herding and it is the same to herd three or four hundred as a thousand and the grass is first class. I intend to stay here till next summer. He is a married man and they are nice people'.

He is still at the Culebra ranch two months later but the going is rough for him. He has had what he describes as the 'chills and fever' but 'kept up with the sheep all the time . . . The winter is colder than usual, the wind is in the north all the time, so it is cold and wet and when wet the ground is awfully disagreeable: it sticks to your shoes so that you can hardly walk.'

Some imagination is needed to realise how much he must have suffered. In the cold and wet and stricken with fever, he continued caring for his thousand sheep, sleeping in the open beside them, cooking on a camp fire in the sticky mud, alone in the wilderness.

In that loneliness and depressed by illness, he adds a postcript which shows how strongly the attractions of the life he had left behind in Wales now appeared to him as day after day this truly heroic young man (he was twenty five) shivered in the cold and wet of the Edwards Plateau in an unusually harsh winter.

> P.S. I am thinking very often of old places there, Heolbank and Mynydd Dimlaith. How I should like to have a walk there on Sunday and have a good dinner on Sunday and a glass of beer and bread and cheese and very often I picture you going to chapel and how I should like to go with you.

173

A word about these Welsh attractions! Heolbank is the lane leading from the village to the farm. It runs along the warm, south face of a hill and commands along its whole length a fine view of the valley, with its meandering river, three railways (at that time) and, in the middle of the valley, only three miles away the market town of Caerphilly, dominated by the walls and towers of its famous 13th century castle.

Mynydd Dimlaith is the mountain that rises from the stream that runs fast and clear in front of the farmhouse whereon, no doubt, he herded his father's sheep and learned his skills as a shepherd.

The beer would have been home-brewed, the bread home-made, baked in a wall oven, heated by the dying embers of wood, and the cheese also was home-made, the well-known Caerphilly cheese.

Even the chapel services had, in retrospect, a heart-warming image as he recalled under the Texan night sky the soul-stirring singing at Hephzibah Welsh Baptist Chapel, especially of those hymns that had been set to music by Welsh composers, and the warm fellowship with farmer-neighbours that followed.

For although William had chosen a way of life that more than any other I can think of entailed a companionless existence, he was not misanthropic, but liked the company of others, and although he lived for years a wanderer in the vast open spaces of south-western Texas, and carried a gun, he was well-read, sensitive and highly responsive to the influence of the Welsh culture in which he had been reared, particularly as expressed in poetry and song, as was his youngest brother, Henry, (a minor poet—Harry o'r Cwm), whom I remember as a staunch supporter of the National Eisteddfod. Dwelling thus on the past, I can't imagine William, even in his worst bouts of sickness and depression, looking for comfort, pleasure and companionship of one sort or another in the saloons of San Antonio or San Angelo, and he was too faithful a shepherd to abandon his flock and take the next boat home. Although conditions on the frontier made observance of the fourth commandment impossible, I'm sure he kept the seventh.

His intention to remain in the Helotes area for the winter was soon abandoned for reasons which he explains in his next letter, dated Feb. 16, 1881. It is written from Miguel, Frio County.

> Now I am altogether on my own hook. I brought my sheep down here for the winter ... about sixty miles south of where I was last ... the reason—the scantiness of the grass up there as there were over three thousand sheep on the ranch (the Culebra ranch, near Helotes), so I did not like to risk them there.

174

A man bought sheep there last winter and kept them there and he lost over one hundred and no doubt hundreds have died there this winter as it has been much colder then usual.

My sheep have done first rate. I camped on a creek about two miles from any house and I run my sheep in the bush most of the time when it was cold and on the prairie when it was fine. I went to the store and Post Office every two weeks.

Now I have moved on to another creek for lambing as it is mostly prairie here. I am eleven miles from the store. The sheep will begin lambing about the 20th (Feb.) and will be through in a month.

The wolves are very bad here. I will have to be very careful when lambing else I will lose them.

I was twelve days coming down here. I engaged a Mexican to bring them down with me, but after about four days travelling he went sick and went home to San Antonio and then I had the chills and fever again.

I will explain what the chills and fever are. The first one you get you feel awful cold all through one's body and its impossible to get warm. It will last about four hours.

Then the fever will come till you get awful warm again. The chills would begin about mid-day and about seven o'clock I would be all right.

I used to have them every other day and each one gets harder and harder till I could hardly stand up.

When I was at Culebra I took quinine and that did break them or stop them for a while but when I began travelling I had them worst than ever till I had them every day. It makes one awful discouraged.

So I had another medicine which made a thorough cure and I have been in first rate health ever since.

I have lived a hard life this winter, slept out every night. I had a couple of blankets and a waggon sheet and I always wear a belt of cartridges with a good frontier revolver.

I intend to shear my sheep at Culebra Ranch and then I am off for Concho which is over two hundred and fifty miles from here. The sheep do first rate by travelling as we don't drive them but go on grazing all the way.

Concho is much better sheep country than this and is much healthier and the land is much cheaper and more room.

I had the Seren Cymru ('The Star of Wales', a Welsh Baptist newspaper) and the Penny Illustrated which I have read about half a dozen times.

Now for Thomas's questions. (Thomas was a younger brother). Yes, there are a good many rivers to cross . . . the drought was then in Texas but I had to pull my clothes off to go through some. I knew by the map what point Concho was and I had a compass. I was on a road sometimes and sometimes no road. The price of land at Concho is from fifty cents to one dollar per acre and they rent at what the tax is, abouty fifty cents on one hundred dollars.

The grass in Western Texas is all wild grass, different from the grass there (Wales). The grass here is coarse long grass, too long for sheep although there is many kinds. At Concho it is mostly musquite grass, which is short grass and does not grow higher than seven or eight inches, something like the mountain grass there (Wales) and is much better for all kinds of stock.

175

Most of the land is sandy and flat, in some places for miles, and rolling hills. There are no high mountains. In some places it is brush but the most is open prairie.

When I came down from San Antonio the rivers were up. One river, the Llano, was very high. I stripped to get through. Horses could not cross it but I could swim first rate. I went till I was in the middle and then the water went too strong for me and took me down and I landed on the same side as I went in so I had to give it up that day.

Yes, I used to come in every night at Culebra.

What sort of family? He is a Yankee, that is he is from New England, six states that is in South Eastern North America. They call them Yankees, and she is a Texan.

I have no dog at all. There are no good dogs here but I wish I could get a dog from there (Wales). I saw two Scotchmen in Uvalde. They had two dogs sent them from home and they had pups which they sold for fifty dollars per head and they used to have a cheese now and then.

Excuse my bad writing as I have to write by the waggon. So I must conclude with kind love.

Apart from its first paragraph acknowledging the receipt of letters, I have quoted the letter in full as it reveals more than what was happening to the young shepherd: it is also a social document portraying what life was like on the Texan prairie before roads linked the various small settlements. He found his way from place to place by map and compass.

Of some significance, too, is his failure to mention towns and what was going on in them. San Antonio and, later, San Angelo, were to him only places where he could post and receive letters and replenish his supply of food and cartridges. He mentiones Uvalde only as the place where he met two Scots with whom he discussed dogs and cheese!

No letter survives, if one was ever written, reporting on his two hundred and fifty miles trek with his flock, which, with the lambs born in Frio County, was now twice as large, possibly numbering about eight hundred. He had planned to halt at Culebra Ranch, near Helotes, a little north of San Antonio, to do his shearing (which indicates that he was on good terms with the 'Yankee' owner and his Texan wife in spite of his deserting them for more favourable winter pasturage further south) and allowing two weeks or so for his time there, the journey would have taken him at five miles a day (he took twelve days for the sixty miles from Culebra to San Miguel) nine weeks at least, possibly as much as three months.

However, on June 18, 1881, just four months later, writing from San Angelo, he tells his mother that he had arrived there on June 6, but not a word about his marathon accomplishment, for such it seems to me

176

when I think of him for almost four months leading his sheep north-
wards over the almost trackless plain, his horse and waggon carrying his
simple needs, and sleeping out night after night with his sheep under
the stars.

The letter, thus ignoring the recent past, is a plea to his mother to lend
him a further £100 'to buy some ewes and rams' and he promises to 'pay
interest on it as on the rest' he had had, which, as represented by his
flock, doubled in numbers by lambs, had already nearly doubled in
value.

He was confident that he could do even better because he was 'staying
steady in one place and not travelling about.' He defines that place as his
camp 'on North Concho River, nine miles from town, San Angelo,' and
adds 'the fort (Fort Concho) is about a quarter of a mile from the town.'

The owner of the land on which he had pitched his camp had made an
offer to sell it or let it, three hundred and twenty acres, for which the
rent would be six cents per acre as it was 'good land where there is
plenty of water.'

He felt that the rent of $19.20 was a good proposition though there
was 'plenty of land in Tom Green (County)' on which he 'could keep
one hundred thousand sheep without paying a cent' but there was no
water on it: indeed, one could 'travel for twenty miles or more without
seeing a drop of water.'

His letter ends:

> I want to go to town for provisions tomorrow so I must be there at daylight and
> will be back in about one hour and a half after as my horse will be fresh now . . .
> Your affectionate son,
>
> William Davies,
> San Angelo

The first part of the next letter is missing, but from what follows the
missing sheet, it can be surmised that his mother, in lending the further
£100 requested, had pleaded with him to return home, which he
counters with,

> 'To come back now would be throwing away a fortune. What would I do back
> there? . . . By and by I will have raised one thousand lambs and they will be
> worth nearly one thousand pounds, saying nothing about the wool'.

And then he breaks into rhetoric, very like that used by Welsh
preachers in the sing-song of the 'hwyl', which needs to be heard to be

177

appreciated, and as what he says is, in effect, a song in praise of Texas I will give it in verse form:

> 'In this part are the best men in Texas
> In this part are the richest men in Texas
> And in this part are the roughest men in Texas
> Stockmen are the richest men in Texas
> Sheepmen out here are the steadiest men you could see and making money faster than any man in the world I believe except the big capitalists.'

He goes on to describe the roughest men in Texas:

> 'All the shepherds and cowboys out here work till they get a little money, then they go to town to spend it; after they spend every cent they go out to work again.'

As for himself, he is reassuring, telling his mother that he still loves his native land and quotes in Welsh a verse of a song in praise of Wales, the last line of which reads 'Ein Walia gwlad y gan' (our Gwalia the land of song).

He had settled now near San Angelo and the next letter is dated February, 1883. Almost certainly there must have been others but he apologises for not writing sooner. This one, again, calls for quotation almost in full for what it says about an unusually cold Texan winter and his manner of life.

> The winter is about over the grass is beginning to grow. It has been a cold winter and lasted about four months, and half of that time like summer there (Wales) and the other half cold wind.
>
> Once we had two inches of snow and it lasted three days. I have been in good luck with the sheep this winter. My loss has been about one head to every one hundred head. Some people have lost very heavily. One man here lost one thousand head in three cold days . . .
>
> I live in my old cabin where I was last winter, and it is very comfortable . . . built of stone and thatched with bur grass. There is a chimney and mantelpiece, everything complete. It is about twelve feet by twelve and big enough. I can stand by the fire to cook and reach everything without moving. It would kill a man to cook same as you cook there if he had to walk to another room for everything.
>
> I got some apples boiling for about an hour here. I eat apple sauce always, every meal, instead of cakes and pudding, less trouble to cook. And beef is cheap, the cheapest meat one can buy, about six cents per pound, bacon about twenty cents per pound.
>
> Henry asks what was the meal I had for Jim Bridge the assessor. I had a rarity for that occasion . . . frogs and grasshoppers stewed and they were delicious . . .
>
> It wants about one hundred good young men for shepherds, wages twenty five dollars per month and board and that is as much as a man can get anywhere in the US.

He wrote again on April 29 and July 17, 1883. This second letter is so packed with information about conditions in the San Angelo area of a hundred years ago, with facts about his flock and fun—yes, fun—that omission of any of it would be a loss of some tidbit for someone. So it must stand as written by the twentyeight-year-old sheepman-fortune hunter.

San Angelo,

Dear Mother,   July 17, 1883

I received your letter of the 14th instant and was glad to hear from you. San Angelo Post Mistress takes good care of my letters, but somehow your letter must be there two weeks before I had it. I go to town almost once a week.

You ask if I am thinking of coming home and say it is a dangerous place to live in. I think I'll take a trip home bye and bye but it will be a short visit. I can't stay long because I will not have made my fortune.

If I don't take a trip home before long, I will not come for years till I have made my fortune, and then when I come I'll come for good.

You say there is a good many murders here. Yes, there is a good many in America but there is about so many in that country (the U.K.). It is as safe here as it is there, if not safer, but for money it is much safer here. I have not been in a house here yet where they lock the door at night.

This part is nothing to what it was two years ago. Now there is a five pound fine for carrying a pistol. It is a thing not wanted in this country at present. I think that country (Wales) is much worse than this. Do the people get drunk as they used to and fight? Is there many robbers around there now? I am a little afraid to come over there now—perhaps they would take me for a stranger!

Is there many poachers there now? Would it be safe for me to come home about eight or nine o'clock at night along Heol-y-bank (the winding lane along the hill side linking his home with the village). I remember that used to be a deuced place—the devil used to live there. Would it be best when I come to buy a couple of good pistols?

You think it best for me to sell the old ewes. I could do that but it is best to keep them along. If I sell them I would only get about $2.50, the same as I gave for them, but if I will keep them only one year they will raise lambs worth $3.50 per head and many will give me extra lambs, so you see it is much better to keep them if they only live one year.

They only shear two and half pounds of wool while their lambs shear five pounds and much better quality. Five men, Mexicans, sheared my sheep. They sheared them in five days. I had to pay 6 cents per hear and board. It was a six month's clip. Weighed a little over a ton.

It went to San Antonio in a waggon, five-mule team. It was twelve days going down. After four days there it sold at satisfactory price. Most of it fetched 21 cents per pound. One sack for 14 cents, two sacks for 18 cents. It averaged 19 cents per pound. I had sorted it into three grades.

My sheep now number between one thousand two hundred and one thousand three hundred head.

It is nice weather now, pretty warm but not as hot as in June . . . Now there is a strong cool breeze always.

I sent my picture to the ones who wanted them. I did not know you wanted one. I had a good picture from A. Davies, Ty-yn-y-Wern some time ago . . . Who is the widow of S. Rees? Is Sam Bachgen Betty (Sam son of Betty) dead?

So I conclude with kind love,

From your affectionate son.

William's attempt to allay his mother's fears concerning his safety is marked by gentle banter. To have told the truth would have worried her deeply and I'm sure she never heard the story that, in response to my boyish curiosity, I had coaxed out of him in that Welsh harvest field thirty years later.

In 1917 Wild West films were beginning to appear in the cinemas and I loved them. But were they true? I put the question to him.

'True enough,' he said.

'Did you see any gun fights, Uncle William?'

'No, but I heard them.'

How he came to hear them without seeing them was explained by the fact that they were almost always fought by drunken men inside saloons into which he never went, but occasionally, when in San Angelo or San Antonio for provisions or to collect and send letters, he had seen cowboys and others stampeding through the swing doors of saloons to get out of the way of bullets being fired inside, just as in the films.

'Did they kill each other?'

'Not often, but they sometimes killed those who did not get out quickly enough. They were too drunk or excited to shoot straight.'

'Were you ever shot at, Uncle William?'

'Yes, once.'

'Were you hit?'

'No.'

'Why not?'

'I think they wanted to frighten me, not kill me.'

Alone with his flock of sheep he had made camp at dusk under a tree, and was sitting by his fire when along a distant skyline he saw the figures of horsemen. As they descended the slope he lost sight of them in the darkness and became aware of their approach only when he heard their horses galloping and bullets hitting the ground around him. Dashing for what little protection the tree could give him he stood behind it as the trigger-happy horsemen went on shooting while riding by. He had not seen them in the dark nor had they said anything.

180

'Why did they do it?'

'They were cattlemen and this was their way of telling me to take my sheep off that land.'

This incident, I feel sure, must have happened when bringing his flock up from Frio County to Fort Concho, a distance of two hundred and fifty miles, as he would have known the boundaries of any territory claimed by the cattlemen in Tom Green County. The cattlemen's preferred manner of argument was with the gun, and though he carried a gun he would not use it if he could avoid doing so.

He was probably telling the truth when he said he had 'not been in a house here yet where they lock the door at night'. Among his other stories that day was that when he left his 'old cabin' on the prairie, sometimes for many days, leading his sheep from one pasturage to another and sleeping out among them, he never locked the place up and on his return was never surprised to discover that it had been occupied by a traveller who had helped himself to provisions, but never without leaving something in recompense—money or other supplies. He said this was an unwritten law of the prairies and its observance impressed him deeply.

He wrote again four months later. He had just finished another shearing, but not of all the flock, 'only nine hundred and fifty head and only four months growth, averaging two pound per head'. The letter proceeds:

> Besides this letter, I send you a newspaper in which I enclose a rattlesnake (he means its tail) which I killed yesterday. He was five feet in length and as stout as my arm. The first thing they do when a man is coming close to them, they coil themselves up, then they hold their heads up about a foot from the ground and rattle their tail. If within reach they spring. They can't spring more than their length, then they coil up again.
>
> They've got very large flat heads. In their upper jaw they've got two teeth just the same as a cat's claws only twice as large; in their lower jaws, many small teeth. They are very poisonous but they won't bite before they are mad and when mad they tell with their tail . . .
>
> I have not seen harvest or ploughing nor hedges for a long time.

His mother had suggested that he should send the money he had saved over to Wales for safe custody as she had no confidence in American banks, but he tells her that American banks are as safe as banks at home.

Better still, he would prefer to invest any money saved in the purchase of land which he believed was sure to appreciate in value, as it had done in the four years he had been in Western Texas.

181

'When I came here,' he said, 'land on the river (Concho) was selling for fifty cents, now for $2.'

He followed this two months later with a Christmas letter beginning 'Fy annwyl mam' (Welsh for my dear mother) which must have gladdened her heart, for after the homely greeting he goes on to tell her that he 'was never in better health ... the weather is splendid, the sheep are doing first rate' and that he has had 'good sport shooting partridges.'

He had also bought 'a splendid cheese' weighing thirty five pounds and costing 'as many shillings'.

Whether the purchase of that huge cheese, which must have formed the staple of many of his meals over the following weeks, stirred in him fond memories of the delicious Caerphilly cheese made by his mother, or, whether romantic visions coloured the lonely vigils with his flock on the Texan prairie, or for other reasons unstated in the surviving letters, William returned home soon afterwards and married Rose Morgan, daughter of the landlord of the Ty-yn-y-Pwll Inn, at his home village of Bedwas.

He brought her back to Texas, no doubt with deep misgivings on the part of her parents, to whom stories out of Texas in those days indicated a lawless land and particularly perilous for a young and lovely bride.

That Rose was both young and beautiful is attested by a photograph taken in San Angelo in 1889, by which time she was the mother of two very young children.

The isolated and ill-equipped shepherd's shack which William had found convenient as a bachelor was no place for a young bride unused to loneliness and hardship, so from their arrival back in Texas, Rose lived within the comparative safety of San Angelo.

On Jan. 5, 1887 writing from Sherwood, Tom Green County, William informs his mother that he had bought a ranch 'eight miles from Sherwood and thirty eight from San Angelo.'

Sherwood is described as a little town of 'about twenty houses, one store and a blacksmith's shop and post office, school and church.'

Almost immediately he is offered an adjoining six hundred and forty acre ranch with a 'good house and well' set, he says, 'nearly at the head of a long valley about nine miles long and three miles wide. The valley begins at the river and runs up west, with middling high hills on each side.' The price: two dollars an acre.

He hasn't quite enough money to complete the purchase and asks his mother for a loan of £60 ($300 then) on which he promises to pay interest at 5%, against the 24% which he tells her he would have to pay

The valley 'with the middling high hills on each side.' A snapshot taken by Dr. Escal F. Duke in 1982

on a loan from a San Angelo bank. The money came quickly, the purchase was completed, and William is delighted by his good fortune.

He reports that the windmill-powered well was capable not only of supplying household needs but also those of the sheep, who in summer drank about two thousand gallons a day, and, by irrigation, the demands of the thirsty vegetable garden which he soon set about planting, for which William requests his mother to send him 'some turnip seeds' as the Texan variety were 'not bigger than potatoes'.

It all sounds idyllic, but whether the isolation necessitated it—he says there was no one else living in the valley—or the risk to life from marauders, or both these and other factors, such as the need for medical help in the births of the children Rose was soon to bear, family legend and later letters combine to suggest that she and her children continued to live 'in town', that is San Angelo.

It must not be inferred from this that Rose was a coward; in her contributions to the letters home at this time she is firm in rejecting pleas from her parents and William's mother to return to the security of Bedwas. Her place, she says, was at William's side, until what he had come to Texas for had been accomplished.

In almost every letter from Sherwood, mention is made of a girl called Lillie. In the letter of Jan. 5th 1887 she is said to be 'in school at San Angelo ever since September.' All references to her indicate that she was treated as a member of the family. They also suggest that she was known to the family at Cwm Farm and I assumed that Rose had taken a younger sister to Texas with her for company. In 1984, however, my own Aunt Lillie, a niece of William, informed me, in her 100th year, that Lillie was Lillie Bartlett, who had gone out from Wales to Texas with William and Rose as a companion-help to Rose in her isolation. What happened to her afterwards my aunt could not remember.

Their letters now bear every mark of ambition well on the way to being satisfied, with every prospect pleasing. As early as November, 1887, William was able to write to his brother Henry reporting that they had 'got a good ranch now. It consists of five sections of land, three thousand two hundred acres . . . we own two sections and we lease three sections from the State at four cents per acre a year.'

On the weather, he said they had had more rain in the preceding two months than in the preceding two years and comments, 'they say it is feast or famine in Texas always . . . we have had enough famine and we are going to have a feast now.'

The sheep were doing well and he was constructing a large dipping vat, 16ft. by 2ft. and 4ft. deep, and he had three thousand two hundred and twenty four pounds of wool in San Angelo awaiting sale.

The same happy note rings through a letter of Feb. 25, 1888. They had plenty of grass and the windmill over the well was 'throwing up plenty of water.'

So it had taken only nine years, since that day in 1879 when William landed at New York, for him to become a successful farmer on a ranch which, by his own account, seems to have been ideally situated for his flocks and himself, if not for his wife and babies.

The next letter reveals how high a price in hardship and anxiety William and Rose had to pay to maintain their hard won prosperity.

184

Dated March 3, 1889, it is headed Sherwood. Written by Rose to her mother-in-law, it begins,

> 'I received a letter from home last week telling us that you were in awful trouble about William. I guess you have heard by this time he is all-right. I was in great trouble about him and could not understand where he was so long. He promised to come into town for Christmas and never came until the 25th January, the reason he did not come was the sheep started lambing.
>
> He had over two hundred head of lambs. Never expected any, so it was impossible for him to come. If he had he would have lost most of the lambs and he knew I was all-right.'

Blessed with modern methods of communication, it is almost impossible to imagine how it was that one hundred years ago a desperately anxious wife could not get in touch for a whole month with her missing husband who might not have been more than fifty miles away, although no one could be expected to know in which direction on the open prairie he had taken his flock for grazing and shelter in that mid-winter.

It is equally difficult to imagine even the most devoted shepherd foregoing Christmas with wife and baby sons for the sake of two hundred lambs, and not only did he absent himself for Christmas but also for the New Year and twenty five days following.

Did he do so in order to avoid some financial loss? Or, as a good shepherd, did he feel he had to be with his sheep when they most needed his care and protection? Remembering this gentle, soft-spoken man, I am persuaded that he could not bring himself to forsake his flock at that time, when wolves would have been an ever present hazard.

He knew, or hoped, that his wife, as she puts it, was 'all-right.' But he cannot have imagined the agonized fears that must have torn her heart, alone with two babies, night and day for a whole month. She must have communicated her fears to her parents and through them, perhaps unwittingly, to William's mother, brothers and sister.

Her letter continues:

> 'They (her mother and father) want us to give up here and come home. Mother is very anxious for us to, but we couldn't think of it now. We have lived here through a hard time since I am out here and are beginning to make money. We expect to have five hundred pounds ($2,500) for wool this year and we made eight hundred lambs last year . . . We have over four hundred now and two thousand three hundred grown sheep. We have had one great loss . . . lost all our bucks, the wolves killed them all. William says he is going to have all South Down bucks now to have big mutton.'

William's compulsive devotion to his lambing ewes and their lambs at a time when his absence would have meant suffering for them (much like that of a captain of a ship when in danger) was repaid as, writing eight weeks later, on April 30th 1889, he reported that his two flocks were doing well, with over nine hundred lambs, and the weather 'everything one could wish for, plenty of grass and water.'

He was then employing Mexican 'herders,' one to each flock, each herder receiving $18 per month and board and 3½ cents per head for shearing.

There was no longer any need to send his wool to San Antonio, as San Angelo had 'become a pretty good wool market,' and he was expecting to get from fifteen to eighteen cents per pound.

He is doing so well that he can foresee the possibility of selling his flocks and ranch 'in a few years if all be well, then (as he puts it) we shall return to the 'Hen Wlad fy nhadau sydd yn annwyl i mi',' that is to the land of my fathers, so dear to me, the first line of the Welsh National Anthem.

On July 9th 1889, William began, and Rose continued and finished, a letter from San Angelo where they had been marooned by rain for two days. William's comment on the weather was: 'When it does anything here, it does it well. When it's dry, it's dry. Now it's wet and people are beginning to get tired of the rain.'

Rose adds that one of the reasons for their being 'in town' was to have their photograph taken as a family group, but the incessant downpour had made it impossible for them to go out and William was anxious to get back to his sheep. However, then or soon afterwards, they did get to the studio for the photograph already mentioned.

It is before me as I write: a handsome couple, seated, stylishly and apparently expensively dressed according to the fashions of those days, the two little boys in clothes hardly distinguishable from those worn by little girls, and Lillie, Rose's Welsh companion standing between and slightly behind the parents. That this could be the hard riding, hard living shepherd, whose bed was a blanket under the night sky a few years before, is barely credible.

There is no reference in any letter to attendance at church or to any sort of social activity, possibly because in those days Sherwood and San Angelo offered little opportunity for either.

William had been accustomed to attending a Baptist Chapel at least twice on Sundays at home, where the services were conducted in Welsh; by nature a shy man, he would have needed every ounce of his large

William and Rose Davies with their sons, William and Horace, and Rose's Welsh companion, Lillie Bartlett, taken in San Angelo in 1889

natural store of courage to cross the threshold of a church where the practices and language were foreign to him. It is also possible that from the very beginning they did not intend to put down roots into the soil of western Texas.

The letters are almost free also of political references. However, in July, 1889, William writing from San Angelo, after expressing satisfaction at the price he had just got for five tons of wool (20½ cents per pound), declares his belief that 'wool is likely to keep up now for the next four years so long as the Republicans are in office,' which suggests that while sheep farmers should vote Republican, wool users would do well to vote Democratic.

There is a further gap in the letters of two years until June 1891, when the last letter to survive was written. William says he was writing it in the San Angelo post office to which he had obviously hastened to dispatch as quickly as possible a letter of condolence to his mother.

He had just heard of the death of his brother, Thomas, at the age of thirty four, which left only one son, Henry, still at home. John, the eldest, was still in Minnesota. His brother's death had converted William's intention to return home into determination to do so, and he promises his mother that 'it will take only a short time before I will be there.'

By this time William's youngest brother, Henry, had taken over the family farm at the Cwm, and Thomas a neighbouring farm, Glyn Rhymney, and it was to Glyn Rhymney that William and Rose returned soon after Thomas's death.

After a few years, during which they added considerably to their family, they took over the ownership and management of the Ty-yn-y-Pwll Inn, Bedwas, from Rose's mother.

Anyone seeing the inn today for the first time would have great difficulty imagining its setting eighty years ago. Not that the inn itself has changed much outwardly: it is still recognizable as the same place that I knew as a boy when it stood, surrounded by fields, beside the the narrow road between Caerphilly and Machen.

For company it had only a tiny turn-pike toll-house opposite which conferred on the inn the name by which it was commonly known 'The Old Pike,' Ty-yn-y-Pwll (meaning literally The House in the Pool) being too much of a mouthful!

In making this move to an inn, William and Rose were doing much the same as his brother, John, and his wife had done in buying and running the Transit House Hotel near St. Paul, Minnesota. In neither case was there any need to look to innkeeping for income. In the case of William and Rose I believe that she had a sentimental attachment to the 'Old Pike', as she had spent much of her girlhood there and it did offer plenty of accommodation for their large family.

After a few years, however, they decided to have a house built and unfortunately chose a site within half a mile of the pub—unfortunately, because about the same time a colliery company decided to sink a pit about a mile away and built a village for the miners between the pub, and the site of the new house. It is a hideous village of seemingly identical houses joined together in terraced streets arranged geometrically to form a right-angled grid, and without any regard for

188

amenity: an ineradicable scar on a formerly pleasant part of a green and, if not beautiful, at least an attractive valley. I'm sorry that the name given to the new development, Trethomas, is attributable to a member of my mother's family who had a large interest, possibly a controlling one, in the colliery company.

The house that William built was named Nantgoch (Red Brook) after the stream that runs near. It is there still, a large and outwardly attractive Edwardian house, which in William's time had some farm land adjoining on which he grazed his horses and made hay for them.

Here he lived in apparent contentment on the rewards of his Texan enterprise, a country gentleman, often to be seen driving his horse and carriage to Caerphilly or Newport, accompanied by his wife and one or more of his four daughters.

He and Rose had one great anxiety in those years; Horace, the second son, born in Texas in 1888, had become an engineer and was working for Krupps in Germany when the 1914-18 War began and was interned in the notorious Ruhleben camp for the whole of World War 1.

Their eldest son, William Edward, after emigrating to Canada, returned to Europe as a soldier in the Canadian Army and fought in the same war and, unscathed, returned to Canada and to his employment with the Royal Bank of Canada at Montreal.

Another son, John, remained in Wales and served for many years as a doctor with the Ministry of Pensions in Cardiff before becoming Superintendent of the Rookwood Hospital at Llandaff.

It is vain to speculate whether William would have done better to have remained in Texas: the call which he felt to return to the 'land of his fathers' was too insistent and was probably felt even more by his wife who, in the conditions of a century ago, could not share his life on the range. He had said in one of his letters that any would-be immigrants from Wales following him to Texas should do so, not individually, but as a group to form a 'colony.'

If such a colony had been established at Sherwood, fostering the distinctive culture of the Welsh, the Davieses might have remained there, for it is plain that over the years of danger, toil and hardship, he had developed a sort of love-hate relationship with his own, private Texas valley where he had established his ranch and part-time home, thus changing it from wilderness to a land, which, if not flowing with milk and honey, at least to a place where sheep could safely graze in green pastures.

The 'Upper Davies Mill' with water tank, located on the site of the Davies Ranch headquarters. The metal windmill has replaced the wooden structure erected by William.   A snapshot taken by Dr. Escal F. Duke in 1982

Postscript

'A place where sheep could safely graze in green pastures!' This was how I imagined Uncle William's Texas domain at his departure and had confidently assumed that the description still applied. The revelation that I was hopelessly wrong in this assumption I owe to Dr. Escal F. Duke, who, until his retirement, was Professor of History at the University of San Angelo. I am indebted to him also for other research into the Davies saga.

He discovered that William did not sell his freehold and leasehold interests in his Texan lands when he and his family, in accordance with the promise made to his mother, returned to Wales shortly after his brother's death, but deferred doing so until 1894 when he returned to Texas for that purpose: a fact I have since confirmed from family sources. The extent of those interests was considerable even by Texan standards, Dr. Duke having found that he had owned or leased seventeen sections, roughly eleven thousand acres.

Dr. Duke also discovered the site of the Davies homestead. I say site because all that remains is the well mentioned in the letter of January 5th, 1887, which continues to function, and is still known as the 'Upper Davies Mill', although the original wooden windmill has been replaced by a metal one.

Changed also is the whole appearance of the area and William's natural paradise is no more. His 'river' is now a dried-up river bed. Gone also are the 'green pastures' which have been invaded and conquered by 'cedar, mesquite and other kinds of underbrush.' The ecology of the whole area has been transformed, visually and agriculturally for the worse, but financially into a bonanza.

For the land on which William's sheep could safely graze is dotted with numerous oil wells, and Dr. Duke observed that had the Davies family remained they could now be Texan oil tycoons.

On the whole, however, I'm inclined to think they did well to get out before that fate overtook them. Enough is enough, and William, Rose and their children lacked nothing.